www.PrincetonReview.com

MATH SMART JUNIOR

Math You'll Enjoy!

by Marcia Lerner, Doug McMullen Jr., Carolyn Wheater,
and The Staff of The Princeton Review

3rd Edition

Random House, Inc.
New York

The Princeton Review, Inc.
2315 Broadway
New York, NY 10024
Email: bookeditor@review.com

ISBN 978-0-375-42869-2

Publisher: Robert Franek
Editor: Laura Braswell
Executive Director of Production: Scott Harris
Senior Production Editor: M. Tighe Wall

Printed in the United States of America.

10 9 8 7 6 5 4 3 2 1

INTRODUCTION

A Very Sneaky Thing

We have done a sneaky thing. In a silly story about three kids—kids who might be a bit like you—we have hidden math problems. Each chapter tells part of the story and covers a different area of math. We assume that you know how to add, subtract, multiply, and divide normal (whole) numbers. Can you calculate $213 - 79$ or $125 \div 5$? If you can do these kinds of math problems, you're ready to start the book. If you *do* have trouble with these kinds of problems, don't sweat it. Just turn to page 211 and do our quick and easy math review. You'll feel much better, and *then* you will be able to plow into the new stuff.

How to Plow

Throughout each chapter are quizzes that let you put what you just learned to use right away. At the end of the book is a section of answers and explanations and a glossary that explains math terms you might not understand. When a word is printed in bold, that word is explained in the glossary.

Wait, there's more!

Before you start you should be prepared to do two things:

- Use scratch paper to solve the problems.
- Have fun.

When you're doing math problems you have to write things down because thinking about numbers can get confusing if you don't. If you take it one step at a time, you'll be amazed at how much you'll know once you reach the end of the book. You may even end up *liking* math. It could happen!

CHAPTER 1

Approximation

"I think my hair is sweating." Jennifer was sprawled, arms flung wide, on the cool grass under the oak that gave One Tree Park its name.

Taylor sat slumped with his back against the tree trunk. "This is unbearable," he moaned. "It's got to be 100 degrees, and it's been this way for months. This weather is never going to break. We're all going to die of heatstroke."

Sondra turned to face him and rolled her eyes. "It was 92 degrees when we passed the bank, and this is the third day of the heat wave." She straightened her back, careful not to brush against the tree. "And the forecast says it will be cooler tomorrow."

Jennifer rolled onto her stomach. "True, but we still have today to get through, and we need to figure out what we can do. I haven't even cooled off yet, and I'm already starting to feel bored."

Taylor winced. "This is the only shade tree in town. We're trapped here."

"Oh, stop it," Sondra said with a little stamp of her foot. "This is not the only shade tree in town. There are plenty of trees in the park down by the river, and more than one oak this size in your front yard."

"Yeah," Taylor sighed, "and come fall, my parents are going to make me rake up all those leaves."

"I seem to remember that your parents gave you extra spending money for doing that job," Sondra pointed out, "so I don't think you ought to complain too much."

"Still," Taylor shrugged, "it's a lot of leaves, and we have more than one tree."

Jennifer flipped onto her back again and studied the oak leaves. "Wouldn't it be cool," she said dreamily, "if you got paid by the leaf?"

"What?" Taylor and Sondra asked at the same instant.

Jennifer seemed to spin in several directions at once, but she came to rest sitting cross-legged facing Taylor. "Wouldn't it be cool if your parents paid you a certain amount per leaf for raking? Even if it was just pennies a leaf—you said it yourself—it's a lot of leaves."

"That would be cool," Taylor agreed. He slid down until he was lying flat on his back, staring up at the tree. After a few minutes, he spoke again. "How in the world could I make that deal with my folks? I'm not going to pick up the leaves one by one to count them. I'd be counting all year."

The three kids were silent for a moment. "You could approximate," Jennifer said.

"Approximate?" Sondra asked, confused.

"Yeah, approximate!" Taylor exclaimed triumphantly.

OOOOOOOOOOOO

Making a logical guess at an amount, such as a length of time, a distance, or the number of leaves on a tree, is called **approximation**. It is an important tool in all kinds of math. When you approximate, you make your best guess. It doesn't have to be exactly right, just reasonably close to the answer. You probably approximate a lot already. If you jump from one rock to another in a stream, you first approximate the distance, and then adjust your jump so that you land on the next rock. If you're going shopping, you might approximate how much your purchases will cost to be certain you have enough money.

Approximation can help you do a lot of things. It can help you check your answers, avoid doing some calculations altogether, and let you work with mathematical ideas without worrying about every computation. Next time you're at lunch with friends, try approximating the time you spend watching television or eating dinner at home.

Approximately how many leaves are on a big oak tree? And how would you ever find out how close your approximation was without actually counting? The truth is you couldn't find out exactly how many leaves are on an oak tree without counting, so unless you've got the time and a ladder, you can't know exactly how close your approximation was. With most math problems, you can't tell how close your approximations are unless you actually do the math, but with experience, your ability to make reasonable approximations will improve. If you're hopping from rock to rock in a stream, first you have to use your senses to make a judgment of how far the distance is, then use your memory of past jumps to decide how much force to put in your legs. If all goes well and your judgment is good, you land on that rock. If not, well, you get wet, but hopefully, your next approximation is better.

With mathematical approximations, the process is similar. The jump is mental, but you do have to use your judgment and past experience. The more practice you get at approximating, the better you'll be at it.

By the way, about how many *glumphs* are in your *bwangko*? If you don't know what a *glumph* or a *bwangko* is, you won't have any idea. (At least we hope not... they're made up words.) But if we tell you that *bwangko* means *mouth* and *glumphs* are *teeth*, you can draw on your experience to make an approximation of the number. So how many teeth are in your mouth? Don't count. Approximate. More than 10? Less than 40? You can count if you want to. Most people don't know how many teeth they have.

Suppose you had to approximate the number of teeth in two people's mouths, or three mouths, or one hundred mouths. Would you count? I hope not. What if you had to estimate how many grains in a cup of sand? You'd be counting a long time on that one, but by using a few simple mathematical operations and just a little counting, you could get you a good approximation. You could count the grains of sand in a teaspoonful—still quite a few—and then find out how many teaspoons are in a cup.

Making an approximation doesn't mean just guessing at any number. When you approximate, you use whole number addition, subtraction, multiplication, and division to find a reasonable number quickly. Those are the operations Jennifer and Taylor are going to use to help them approximate the number of leaves on the oak tree. (You didn't think they were going to count them, did you?) You probably know how to do these operations already, but it's always good to practice, especially without paper and pencil. Mental math will be any important skill throughout your life. If you need help with these operations, you'll find them all in the Review Appendix.

When you're thinking about adding and subtracting, it's often helpful to use a number line. The number line places all the numbers in order along a line, with the smaller numbers to the left and the larger numbers to the right. Numbers on the right are always bigger than numbers on the left.

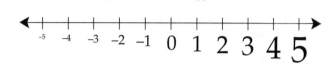

Number lines have arrows on the ends indicating that they continue forever. There is no largest number and no smallest number. Numbers go on forever. Mathematicians say that there are infinitely many numbers, or that the numbers extend to infinity. These mathematicians will use the symbol ∞ to mean infinity, but it's important to remember that ∞ is not a number. When you see the symbol ∞, just remember you're looking at something that goes on forever.

The number line can help you visualize an addition problem. Start with the number you have, then move right to add. The addition problem $2 + 3 = 5$ looks like this on the number line.

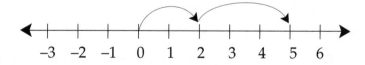

You start from 0, jump 2 spaces right, then jump 3 more spaces to the right, and you end up at 5.

If you do a subtraction problem on the number line, you move left instead of right, because subtraction is the opposite of addition. The problem $5 - 3 = 2$ looks like this.

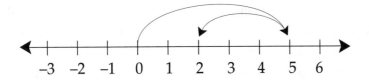

Starting from 0, the first jump to the right takes you to 5, but then you jump 3 units left to subtract, ending up at 5.

THINK ABOUT THIS

Sometimes, you might be asked to answer a math problem that is written out in words. For instance, a problem that says, "If Sondra has 1 hat and Jennifer has 2 hats, how many hats do they have together?" actually means $1 + 2 = ?$ The best way to solve these word problems is to write things down as you go. After every pause in the sentence—when you find out information about Sondra, for example—write down what you know and label it if necessary. This way, you can translate a written sentence into an arithmetic problem easily. Look for clues in the language of the problem that will tell you what operation to use. For example, the word "together" in the problem here tips you off that it is most likely an addition problem.

⊙⊙⊙⊙⊙⊙⊙⊙⊙⊙⊙⊙

"How in the world can you approximate the number of leaves on a tree?" Sondra protested. "How could you know? I mean, there could be..."

"1050," said Jennifer.

"Actually, it's closer to 1,022." Taylor looked across at Jennifer.

"How did you...? What did you...?" gulped Sondra. "I beg your pardon?"

Jennifer propped herself on her elbows and explained. "Well, there are about 5 leaves on every small branch, and there are about 7 small branches on each medium branch. So 7 small branches times 5 is 35. There are 35 leaves on every medium-size branch. Okay?" She didn't wait for an answer. "There are about three medium-sized branches on every big branch. So, if one medium-sized branch is 35, then 3 medium-size branches will be 3 times 35, or 105. That gives us 105 leaves on every big branch. There are 10 big branches and 10 times 105 is 1050, so I figure there are 1,050 leaves on the tree!" Jennifer announced, looking pleased with herself.

Taylor cleared his throat. "I think your estimate may be a little high. If I divide the tree into 9 levels, starting at the top, then the topmost level has 2 leaves." Taylor pointed up to the top of the tree. "The second level down has about twice that, which is 4 leaves. The third level down is twice 4, or 8 leaves. I think it doubles at every level, so the fourth level is 16 leaves, but I have to keep that going for 9 levels. The fifth level is 32 leaves, the sixth is 64 leaves, and the seventh is 128. Level 8 will be 256 leaves and the bottom layer is 512 leaves. Add up $2 + 4 + 8 + 16 + 32 + 64 + 128 + 256 + 512$ and you get 1,022."

Jennifer and Taylor both turned to look at Sondra. "So," Jennifer asked, "who's right?" Sondra looked uneasily at Jennifer, then at Taylor, then back at Jennifer. "Well," she said after a moment, "how about we split the difference?"

"Split the difference?" Taylor asked. "What does that mean?"

"It just means we find a number midway between the two approximations you came up with. We can subtract to find the difference between your estimates. Since $1050 - 1022 = 28$, the difference is 28. Then we split that difference into two parts, and 28 ÷ 2 = 14. The number we want is 14 less than Jennifer's approximation and 14 more than Taylor's guess. Since 1050 − 14 = 1036 and 1022 + 14 = 1036, can we agree that there are approximately 1036 leaves on this oak tree?"

○○○○○○○○○○○○

Sondra's explanation does a good job of making clear what the expression *split the difference* means, but mathematically, what she did was to find the **average**. The average of a group of numbers is found by adding up the numbers and dividing by the number of numbers you have. In this case, Sondra had two numbers, so she could have added 1050 + 1022 to get 2072, and then when she divided by 2, she would have gotten 1036. The average of Taylor and Jennifer's approximations is 1036, the same number Sondra got by splitting the difference.

In working out their approximations of how many leaves were on the oak tree, Sondra, Taylor, and Jennifer didn't use any fancy math. All they did was add, subtract, multiply, and divide, but that doesn't mean the problems they solved were easy. The hardest part of a math problem often is knowing what to do and when to do it. Sondra, Jennifer, and Taylor put their math problems together like real pros. Putting the steps of a math problem together so it makes sense is a valuable skill, and it's one of the things we hope you will learn from this book. First, however, you've got to be able to do the basic operations. If you have any trouble understanding how to do addition, subtraction, multiplication, or division, go to the review appendix for an explanation of (and some practice with) each operation.

CHAPTER 2

Order of Operations

"OK," Taylor said, pulling himself back up to a sitting position, "so we estimate that there are 1036 leaves on an oak tree. Maybe—and that's a big maybe—my parents would agree to pay me by the leaf for raking. That doesn't do anything for us now."

"I'm hungry," Jennifer stated.

"You're always hungry," Sondra said. When Jennifer nodded, Sondra turned to Taylor. "You make it sound like we have some kind of problem," she said.

Taylor jumped up. "We do have a problem. We're trapped under this tree because it's too hot to leave the shade. We're hot, we're sweaty, we're bored...."

"And we're hungry," said Jennifer, getting to her feet.

"Speak for yourself," said Sondra.

"I am," said Jennifer. "How much money do we have?"

Taylor stared at her. "Why?"

"You're bored. I'm hungry. We need to go find some lunch and something to do, and that's going to take some money. I've got..." She dug a hand into the pocket of her shorts and pulled out a crumpled bill and some coins. After studying the collection in her hand for a moment, she finished her sentence. "...$1.94. What about you?"

"I've got $2.50," Taylor said. He peeked in his pocket. "$2.57, actually," he corrected.

Taylor and Jennifer turned to Sondra, who sighed. "OK, OK," she said, "I've got $2.75." Sondra thought for a minute. "That gives us a little more than 7 dollars. Where are you going?" she called after Jennifer, who was striding down the hill. Sondra and Taylor scrambled to catch up with her.

"We're not going to find lunch or something to do sitting here," Jennifer said. "We need to go into town."

"We're not going to find lunch or something to do for 7 dollars in town," Sondra pointed out. Her protest did not slow Jennifer's pace.

"Oh! Do you smell that?" Taylor asked.

The three kids froze in place. "Pizza," Sondra mumbled.

3 1326 00429 8370

"Not just pizza," Jennifer said happily, "Ippolitto's pizza. Come on!" She sprinted across the street, pausing only to allow a tractor-trailer to pull away from the curb in front of Ippolitto's restaurant.

"We can't afford this," Sondra called after her. She and Taylor picked their way around stacks of cartons to join Jennifer at the restaurant's window.

"You kids ready for lunch?" Mr. Ippolitto's deep voice came from behind them. The kids turned to see him smiling at them, and each of them in turn greeted him.

"It smells wonderful, Mr. Ippolitto," Jennifer explained, "but it's not really in our budget."

"Well, would you young people be interested in a job?" Mr. Ippolitto asked.

Taylor elbowed in front of Jennifer, full of curiosity. "A job?"

"Well, I'm a little short-handed today," Mr. Ippolitto explained, "because one of my workers is on vacation and another is sick today." He gestured toward the stacks of cartons on the sidewalk. "You can see I've just gotten a big delivery, and all of this needs to be moved to the storeroom."

"And you'd pay us to do that?" Taylor asked.

"Sure," said Mr. Ippolitto, "it's minimum wage, of course, but I suspect it'll cover your lunches and maybe leave a bit to spare."

"That storeroom wouldn't by any chance be air-conditioned, would it?" Jennifer asked.

"It is," Mr. Ippolitto replied, "and some of the boxes go into the walk-in refrigerator down there."

"We can do that," Sondra said. "We'll divide the work three ways and be done in no time!"

Sondra's suggestion shows enthusiasm, but can they really divide the work three ways? Well, that depends on how many boxes actually need to be moved. The real question is whether the number of boxes is a multiple of 3. Do you remember the quick way to check? If the digits of the number add up to a multiple of 3, then the number is a multiple of 3. If there are 132 boxes, you add $1 + 3 + 2$ and get 6. Since 6 is a multiple of 3, 132 is also a multiple of 3. Would 119 boxes be evenly divisible by 3? Well, $1 + 1 + 9$ is 11 and 11 is not a multiple of 3, so no, 119 is not evenly divisible by 3.

You probably remember other quick tricks for checking divisibility. If a number ends in 0, it's divisible by 10. If it ends in 5 or 0, it's divisible by 5, and if it ends in 2, 4, 6, 8, or 0, it's divisible by 2. A number that is divisible only by itself and 1 is called a **prime** number. The number 19, for example, has no factors except itself and 1. The whole number multiplication problem with an answer of 19 is 1×19, so 19 is prime. On the other hand, 20 is divisible by 2, 5, and 10 (since 20 ends in 0). You can get an answer of 20 by doing 1×20, 2×10, or 4×5, so 20 is not prime.

Taylor walked over and lifted a large carton. "Air-conditioning, here I come!" he said with a smile. "These aren't so heavy."

"Oh! The storeroom has a numeric keypad lock," Mr. Ippolitto said, "and you'll need the access code. If you try to prop the door open, the alarm will sound, so you'll have to enter the code each time you go in." He reached into the pocket of his apron and handed Sondra a small card. It read $63 + 3 \times 5 - 6 \div 2 + 3^2 (5+1)$.

Sondra looked back and forth from the card to Mr. Ippolitto several times. "This is the code?"

Mr. Ippolitto laughed. "The answer to that problem is the code. I figured this way at least anyone who tries to steal the code will have to work for it. Now, if you'll excuse me, I've got to get back to the kitchen. Come up to the restaurant when you're done with those boxes, and we'll get you fixed up with lunch."

"Let's go," said Taylor, shifting the carton he was holding. Jennifer and Sondra each grabbed a box, and the three set off down the alley to the storeroom door. In front of the big steel door they paused, and Sondra looked down at the card in her hand. Jennifer and Taylor looked over her shoulder.

Taylor punched 4 digits into the keypad. "1 – 0 – 2 – 6," he called out as he hit the keys. A hard yank on the door handle nearly knocked him off balance, but the door didn't budge.

Jennifer hid a giggle. "How do you get 1026?" she asked. "It's 21." She cleared the keypad and entered her answer. Taylor tried the door again, more gently this time. It didn't move.

"Wait a second," Sondra said. She mumbled several numbers before making a suggestion. "Try 129." As soon as Jennifer entered the number on the keypad, there was a buzzing sound. Taylor tried the door again, and this time, it opened.

Believe it or not, math and pizza-making have some things in common. You can have all the ingredients, but if you don't put them together in the right order, you can make a real mess. Imagine trying to make a pizza by pouring out the sauce first and then adding the dough! Well, it happens all the time in math because people don't know the "recipe" for the problem. It is called the order of operations.

Here is the problem that Taylor, Jennifer, and Sondra were working on.

$$63 + 3 \times 5 - 6 \div 2 + 3^2 (5 + 1)$$

This problem looks complicated, but there is a specific order, and you always follow it. The order is **Parentheses**, **Exponents**, **Multiplication** and **Division**, **Addition**, and **Subtraction**.

Always do the stuff in the parentheses first.

$63 + 3 \times 5 - 6 \div 2 + 3^2 \overbrace{(5 + 1)}$ becomes $63 + 3 \times 5 - 6 \div 2 + 3^2 (6)$. When you're finished doing what is in the parentheses, you can often drop the parentheses, but we are going to leave them here, because they are serving another purpose as well. They are also telling you to multiply 3^2 times 6.

The next operation is **exponents.** Exponents are those little numbers that tell you how many times a number is multiplied by itself. For example, $4^2 = 4 \times 4$, which is 16. If you had 2^5, that would mean $2 \times 2 \times 2 \times 2 \times 2$.

In this problem, you have 3^2, which is 3×3, or 9, so the problem becomes $63 + 3 \times 5 - 6 \div 2 + 9(6)$.

Multiplication and division are done next. Make sure that you do them *before* doing any addition or subtraction, and work left to right, doing multiplication or division, as you meet them.

$$63 + \overbrace{3 \times 5}^{15} - 6 \div 2 + 9(6)$$

$$63 + 15 - \overbrace{6 \div 2}^{3} + 9(6)$$

$$63 + 15 - 3 + \overbrace{9(6)}^{54}$$

$$63 + 15 - 3 + 54$$

That leaves addition and subtraction. Do them left to right. (You can do it differently once you understand negative numbers, which we'll cover in Chapter 9.)

$$\overbrace{63 + 15}^{78} - 3 + 54$$

$$\overbrace{78 - 3}^{75} + 54$$

$$\overbrace{75 + 54}^{129}$$

$$129$$

How did Jennifer and Taylor get different answers? Well, Taylor tried to just work left to right, without thinking much about the order of operations at all. Jennifer remembered that there was a rule about the order in which you should do things, but she made a common mistake. Lots of people learn the order as parentheses, exponents, multiplication, division, addition, subtraction, and they think that you do all the multiplying before any dividing and all the adding before any subtraction. That's how

Jennifer went wrong. She was doing OK until it was time to add and subtract, but then she tried to jump over the subtraction, instead of working left to right.

$$\left(\overset{78}{\overbrace{63+15}} - \overset{\text{OOPS!}}{\overbrace{3+54}} \right)$$

How can you remember the order of operations? Some people remember the word PEMDAS, others remember the helpful phrase using words that begin with each letter: <u>P</u>lease <u>E</u>xcuse <u>M</u>y <u>D</u>ear <u>A</u>unt <u>S</u>ally. Use whichever one works for you, but remember to do multiplication <u>and</u> division left to right as you meet them, then addition <u>and</u> subtraction left to right as you meet them.

ARITHMETIC CHECK

1. $17 + 34 - 22 = ?$ Is the answer odd or even?

2. $505 - 100 \times 3 = ?$ Is the answer odd or even? Is the answer a multiple of 3?

3. $20 \times 3 \div 4 + 23 - 17 + 83 = ?$ Is the answer odd or even? Is the answer a multiple of 5? Also, is the answer a prime number?

4. $234 \div 6 \times 2 + 103 = ?$ Is the answer a multiple of 5? Divide the answer by 3. What is the final answer now?

5. $200 + 309 \times 25 \div 15 + 10 = ?$ Is the answer a multiple of 5? Is the answer a multiple of 3 or a prime number?

6. Jennifer had 37 autographed baseballs, but she sent 29 to her older brother Harry, who missed playing baseball when he was

away visiting a friend in France. If she doesn't get any new ones, how many autographed baseballs does she have left?

7. Taylor planted a patch of strawberries in his backyard. In June, they were beautiful, ripe, and ready to pick. He went out with a basket and filled it with 27 strawberries. He filled this basket 3 times, until there were no more strawberries. How many strawberries did he pick? Remember to approximate first.

8. Sondra invited 11 friends to her birthday party, and her dad bought 26 ice cream sandwiches. If Sondra and her friends each got an equal number of ice cream sandwiches, how many did each of them get? Were there any left over?

9. Taylor carried 26 loads of books to the library for Ms. Greely, who lived down the street. Each load weighed 251 pounds! (He used a wheelbarrow.) How many pounds of books did Taylor carry?

10. Jennifer got $39 from each of her 14 relatives. She wants to use the money to buy as many maps as possible (she's a real travel buff). Each map costs $15. How many maps can she buy, and will she have any money left over at the end?

Great job! You have mastered the basics. Now check out the answers and explanations, and then see what Jennifer, Taylor, and Sondra are doing in the neighborhood.

CHAPTER 3

Fractions

"Forty-three," Taylor announced and gave a great sigh.

"Forty-three what?" Jennifer wiped the perspiration from her forehead with the back of her hand.

"Forty-three trips, each, from the sidewalk to the storeroom to get the whole delivery moved," Taylor explained.

Sondra estimated quickly. "At least 129 cartons, then—more, since we sometimes took a couple of small ones at a time."

Jennifer walked to the far end of the storeroom. "I hope it was OK for us to stack boxes against this door."

"Well, there was already stuff there, and the door doesn't look like it's been opened in years," Sondra said, "but we can check with Mr. Ippolitto when we go upstairs."

"And let's go upstairs," Taylor said. "I'm starved."

Upstairs was cool and quiet, and it smelled of tomato and garlic. "Ah! You're done!" Mr. Ippolitto greeted them. "Pizza for everyone?"

"I'm as hungry as a horse," said Jennifer.

"I think I could use a nibble or two," said Sondra.

Sondra, Taylor, and Jennifer washed up quickly and settled themselves around a table. Mr. Ippolitto brought over three glasses filled with ice and inquired about what they would like to drink. When they agreed that lemonade would be refreshing, their host called for two pitchers. He used one to fill their glasses, and he left the rest for refills. By the time the kids had quenched the thirst they worked up moving boxes, Mr. Ippolitto had returned to their table with three steamy personal size pizzas and set one in front of each of them. "I thought you might like to cut your own," he said, placing a cutting wheel on the table.

Taylor made the first cut. He cut straight down the middle of the pizza, like this.

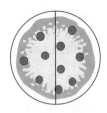

How much of the pizza is each piece? To answer that, you need a fraction. A fraction is a number that is usually used to show a part of something bigger. The whole pizza, at this point in its life, is made up of 2 equal pieces. In a fraction, the bottom number, or denominator, shows how many equal parts make up the whole.

$$\overline{2} \leftarrow \text{whole}$$

One piece of this pizza is 1 part, the number on the top of the fraction, called the numerator.

$$\frac{1}{2} \begin{array}{l} \leftarrow \text{part} \\ \leftarrow \text{whole} \end{array}$$

A fraction shows what part of the whole you have. A piece is one part out of a possible 2 parts. A fraction can also be thought of as a division statement. $\frac{1}{2}$ is what you get when 1 is divided by 2, or divided into 2 equal pieces.

THINK ABOUT THIS

Any number can be written as a fraction by putting it over 1. $5 = \dfrac{5}{1}$, $3 = \dfrac{3}{1}$, $1 = \dfrac{1}{1}$. A denominator of 1 says the whole is in one piece. If you think about it as a division statement, dividing by 1 doesn't change anything. 5 divided by 1 is still 5.

OOOOOOOOOOOO

Taylor made another cut in the pizza, and it looked like this.

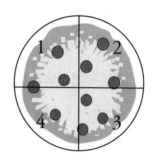

OOOOOOOOOOOO

What would you call one of the pieces of the pizza as it is cut up now? How would you write it down? The piece is 1 part out of a whole of 4 pieces. The piece is $\dfrac{1}{4}$, called one-fourth or one-quarter.

What if you had 2 of these slices?

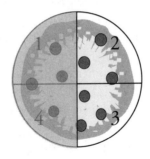

You would have $\frac{2}{4}$, or two-fourths, but you might notice that two-fourths

look like one half. As you can tell from the picture, $\frac{1}{2}$ and $\frac{2}{4}$ are equal.

The same part of a whole can be named by many fractions that look dif-

ferent but are equal.

How could you tell the fractions were equal if you didn't have a picture? How

do you know that $\frac{2}{4} = \frac{1}{2}$? Take a more careful look at $\frac{2}{4}$. Are 2 and 4 divis-

ible by the same number? Sure they are! Both 2 and 4 are even, so they are

divisible by 2. You can divide both the numerator and the denominator

by 2. $\frac{2 \div 2 = 1}{4 \div 2 = 2}$, so $\frac{2}{4}$ becomes $\frac{1}{2}$. Now, 1 and 2 have only one divisor in

common, the number 1, and dividing by 1 doesn't change anything. The

fraction $\frac{1}{2}$ is in simplest form, or lowest terms. Reducing is a way of put-

ting a fraction into its simplest form.

Let's try a few others; $\frac{3}{9}$ says the whole is divided into 9 equal parts and we have 3 of them. Does $\frac{3}{9}$ have a number that divides evenly into both the top and the bottom? Here's another way that knowing your times tables will come in handy. Both 3 and 9 are divisible by 3, so if you divide both the numerator and denominator of $\frac{3}{9}$ by 3, $\frac{3 \div 3 = 1}{9 \div 3 = 3}$. Three parts out of 9 is equal to 1 part out of 3. The fraction $\frac{3}{9}$ is equal to $\frac{1}{3}$, and $\frac{1}{3}$ is in simplest form.

Try $\frac{4}{16}$. What number goes into both the numerator and the denominator? Well, both the top and bottom numbers are even, so try 2. The fraction $\frac{4}{16}$ divided top and bottom by 2 becomes $\frac{2}{8}$. Is $\frac{2}{8}$ in simplest form? No, because 2 and 8 are both even and so both can be divided by 2 again. $\frac{2 \div 2 = 1}{8 \div 2 = 4}$. This fraction is in simplest form, because 1 is the only number that divided both 1 and 4.

If you wanted to, you could have reduced the original fraction by 4 and skipped a step. $\frac{4 \div 4 = 1}{16 \div 4 = 4}$. This is not necessary, and in fact, it is sometimes easier just to go by twos and threes, in small steps, so as not to make mistakes. If you want to, however, you can reduce by larger numbers, as long as they are factors of both the numerator and denominator of the fraction.

The spicy aroma of the freshly cut pizza filled the restaurant. Taylor silently stared at the pizza as though he'd fallen in love. "Hurry up with that cutter," Jennifer prodded. Taylor quickly made 2 more slices across the pizza. It looked like this.

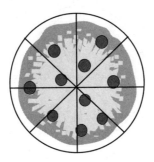

Jennifer snatched the pizza cutter from him and made 3 quick cuts across her plate. Her pizza looked like this.

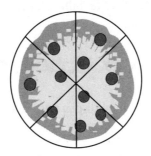

She paused just long enough to pass the cutter to Sondra before she slid a wedge off the plate, folded it, and took a big bite. "Ummm," she murmured in delight.

"Isn't it wonderful?" Taylor agreed. Sondra was still cutting. One cut, then another, and a third, a fourth, and...

"Are you going to eat it or just play with it?" Jennifer asked with her mouth full.

"I prefer smaller pieces," Sondra explained, making cuts 5, 6, 7, and finally 8. Then she set the cutter down on an extra napkin and picked up her knife and fork. Her pizza looked like this.

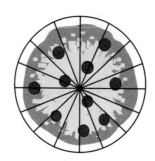

Sondra put a slice of her pizza on a plate, carefully removed the crust, and then cut the rest into tiny, cheesy pieces that she ate with a fork. Taylor ate his pizza slowly, with a look of dreamy satisfaction. Jennifer, however, wolfed hers down so fast that she was into her second piece before anyone else noticed.

OOOOOOOOOOOO

How would you write out the full pizza as a fraction? Taylor's pizza was cut in 8 pieces, so the whole pizza is 8 pieces out of 8, or $\frac{8}{8}$, but Jennifer's pizza was cut in 6 pieces, so the whole pizza is 6 pieces out of 6, or $\frac{6}{6}$. For Sondra, the whole is $\frac{16}{16}$, because she cut her pizza into 16 pieces. Any number over itself makes a fraction equal to 1. The fraction bar means divide, so any number divided by itself equals 1.

THINK ABOUT THIS

Since a fraction bar means divide and you can never divide by 0, the denominator of the fraction can *never* be 0. The denominator of a fraction tells you how many pieces make up the whole. How could the whole be cut into zero pieces?

When Jennifer has eaten 2 pieces of her pizza, what fractional part of her pizza has she eaten? Well, she ate 2 parts out of a whole of 6, so she ate $\frac{2}{6}$ or $\frac{1}{3}$ of her pizza. What part is left? You can see that 4 of the 6 pieces have not yet been eaten, so $\frac{4}{6}$ of her pizza is left. In simplest form, that's $\frac{2}{3}$ of her pizza. To find out how much is left, subtract what was eaten from the whole. Jennifer cut her pizza into sixths and ate 2 pieces, so $\frac{6}{6} - \frac{2}{6} = \frac{4}{6}$.

The trick for adding and subtracting fractions is that you only add or subtract the numerators, and the denominator stays the same. The number of parts making up the whole doesn't change. The number of parts taken or left is what changes.

$$\frac{6 \text{ parts}}{6 \text{ parts in the whole}} - \frac{2 \text{ parts eaten}}{6 \text{ parts in the whole}} = \frac{4 \text{ parts left}}{6 \text{ parts in the whole}}$$

What if you combine what is left with what Jennifer has eaten? $\frac{4}{6} + \frac{2}{6} = \frac{6}{6}$ or 1 whole pizza.

"This is the best pizza I've ever had!" Jennifer said between big, happy mouthfuls. Only 1 slice remained on her plate.

"Delicious, yes, but I believe I've had quite enough to satisfy my appetite," Sondra commented, removing the napkin she'd tucked 'round her collar. There were 4 skinny slices left on her plate.

"Mmmmm," Taylor nodded. "I hate to say it, but I'm feeling pretty good now too." He eyed the 3 wedges on his plate.

Taylor and Jennifer each ate 5 pieces, but their pieces were different sizes. Taylor's pizza was cut into 8 pieces, so he ate $\frac{5}{8}$ of a pizza. Jennifer cut her pizza into 6 pieces so she ate $\frac{5}{6}$ of a pizza. Sondra ate 12 of her 16 pieces. Did she eat more than Jennifer did?

There's a trick you can use to compare 2 fractions. Look at $\frac{5}{8}$ and $\frac{5}{6}$. Write the fractions side by side. Multiply the first denominator times the second numerator and place the answer above the second numerator.

$$\frac{5}{8} \nearrow \overset{40}{\frac{5}{6}}$$

Next multiply the second denominator times the first numerator and write the answer above the first fraction.

$$\overset{30}{\frac{5}{8}} \nwarrow \frac{5}{6}$$

When you've done both calculations, the fraction with the larger floating number is the larger fraction.

$$\overset{30}{\frac{5}{8}} < \overset{40}{\frac{5}{6}}$$

Since 40 is bigger than 30, $\frac{5}{6}$ is bigger than $\frac{5}{8}$. This means that the 5 pieces Jennifer ate $\frac{5}{6}$ are more pizza than the $\frac{5}{8}$ that Taylor ate.

Sondra ate 12 of her 16 pieces. Is that more than Jennifer ate?

$$\overset{80}{\frac{5}{6}} \times \overset{72}{\frac{12}{16}}$$

Since 80 is larger than 72, $\frac{5}{6} > \frac{12}{16}$, Jennifer ate more pizza than Sondra.

How much pizza did the kids eat? It's not enough to talk about how many pieces they ate because each of them cut pieces of a different size. Taylor's pieces were eighths, Jennifer's were sixths, and Sondra's were sixteenths.

If you wanted to figure out how much pizza they ate, in total, you would have to add $\frac{5}{8} + \frac{5}{6} + \frac{12}{16}$. But how can you add fractions that don't have the same denominator?

When fractions have the same denominator, when the pieces are the same size, all you need to do is to add the numerators, the top numbers that tell how many pieces you have. The denominator doesn't change. When the denominators are different, you have to translate each fraction into an equal fraction with a matching or common denominator. Sometimes you can do this easily by changing 1 fraction. For example, Taylor cut his pizza into 8 pieces, while Sondra cut hers into 16 pieces. One of Taylor's pieces is equal to 2 of Sondra's pieces. So the $\frac{5}{8}$ that Taylor ate would be equal to $\frac{5 \times 2}{8 \times 2} = \frac{10}{16}$. Taylor and Sondra together ate $\frac{5}{8} + \frac{12}{16} = \frac{10}{16} + \frac{12}{16} = \frac{22}{16}$. Since 22 is greater than 16, $\frac{22}{16}$ is more than a whole pizza. A fraction that is worth more than a whole is called an improper fraction. This one is made up of a whole, $\frac{16}{16}$, plus another $\frac{6}{16}$. $\frac{22}{16} = \frac{16}{16} + \frac{6}{16} = 1\frac{6}{16}$.

When people talk about fractions that are greater than 1, they don't usually say $\frac{22}{16}$. They are more likely to use a mixed number like $1\frac{6}{16}$. To make a fraction into a mixed number, remember that the fraction bar means divide, and do just that. Divide the numerator by the denominator. If your improper fraction is $\frac{7}{4}$, divide 4 into 7. Since 4 goes into 7 once, 1 will be your whole number. The remainder is 3, and that will go over the denominator to make the fraction part.

$$\frac{7}{4} = 1\frac{3}{4}$$

If you ever want to convert an improper fraction to a mixed number, just divide and put the remainder over the denominator, next to the quotient.

Try another one: $\frac{17}{5}$. Well, 5 goes into 17 three times, with a remainder of 2. The remainder goes over the denominator, which gives you $3\frac{2}{5}$.

To convert a mixed number into a fraction is easy too. Let's try it with $4\frac{2}{3}$. Multiply the denominator by the whole number and add that answer to the numerator. Then put the whole mess over the original denominator, and you get $4\frac{2}{3} = \frac{12+2}{3} = \frac{14}{3}$. Now you have got an improper fraction again.

Why would you want to convert mixed numbers into improper fractions? Well, that's one of the easiest ways to add and subtract them. Change the mixed number to an improper fraction, add or subtract the fractions, and then, if you want, change the improper fraction back to a mixed number.

It can be more difficult to add fractions when the translation to the new denominator is not obvious. Jennifer's $\frac{5}{6}$ and Taylor's $\frac{5}{8}$ need to be translated into a common denominator before they can be added, and there is no easy way to change sixths to eighths or eighths to sixths. The secret is to find a denominator to which both eighths and sixths can translate. Another way to think about that is to find a number that can be divided by both 8 and 6. Any number that is a multiple of both 8 and 6 could be the common denominator, but since most of us don't want to work with numbers any larger that necessary, we try to find the smallest number that will work, the lowest common denominator. So while you could use $6 \times 8 = 48$, the lowest common denominator is 24.

To translate a fraction to an equal fraction with the new denominator, multiply by a disguised one. The number 1 can be written as a fraction by using any non-zero number as both the numerator and the denominator. To translate the $\frac{5}{6}$ to a fraction with a denominator of 24, you want to multiply the 6 on the bottom by 4, so multiply $\frac{5}{6}$ by $\frac{4}{4}$.

$$\frac{5}{6} \times \frac{4}{4} = \frac{20}{24}$$

The fraction $\frac{20}{24}$ is equal to $\frac{5}{6}$. You can be sure of that because you multiplied by 1, and multiplying by 1 doesn't change anything. Now you have a fraction equal to $\frac{5}{6}$, but with the denominator of 24 that you wanted.

To translate $\frac{5}{8}$ to a fraction with a denominator of 24, multiply by 1 disguised as $\frac{3}{3}$.

$$\frac{5}{8} \times \frac{3}{3} = \frac{15}{24}$$

Once the fractions have been translated, you can simply add the numerators.

$$\frac{5}{6}+\frac{5}{8}=\frac{20}{24}+\frac{15}{24}=\frac{35}{24}=\frac{24+11}{24}=\frac{24}{24}+\frac{11}{24}=1\frac{11}{24}$$

The other way to get the fractions to have the same denominator is to use a technique called the bow tie. Remember how we compared fractions by multiplying and comparing the floating numbers? In this case, you multiply in the shape (almost) of a bow tie.

First, multiply up diagonally from the right to the left and write the number over the left side.

$$^{12}\diagdown\frac{3}{8}+\frac{1}{\diagup\!\!\!4}$$

Then, multiply up diagonally from the left to the right and write the number down above the right side.

$$\frac{3}{\diagup\!\!\!8}+\frac{\diagup\!\!\!1}{4}^{8}$$

Then, multiply the 2 denominators and write that product as the denominator of your answer.

$$\frac{3}{8}+\frac{1}{4}$$
$$_{32}$$

$$^{12}\diagdown\frac{3}{\diagup\!\!\!8}+\frac{\diagup\!\!\!1}{\diagup\!\!\!4}^{8}$$
$$_{32}$$

Last add the 2 floating numbers to form the numerator of your answer.

$$=\frac{12+8}{32}=\frac{20}{32}$$

Can you reduce $\frac{20}{32}$? Sure. First, divide the top and the bottom by 2.

$\frac{20}{32} = \frac{10}{16}$. Can you reduce again? Sure. $\frac{20}{32} = \frac{10}{16} = \frac{5}{8}$. Ta da!

So how much pizza did the kids eat? $\frac{5}{8} + \frac{5}{6} + \frac{12}{16}$ will need a common denominator. The smallest number that is divisible by 8, 6, and 16 is 48, so that will be the common denominator.

$$\frac{5}{8} + \frac{5}{6} + \frac{12}{16} = \frac{5}{8} \times \frac{6}{6} + \frac{5}{6} \times \frac{8}{8} + \frac{12}{16} \times \frac{3}{3}$$
$$= \frac{30}{48} + \frac{40}{48} + \frac{36}{48}$$
$$= \frac{30 + 40 + 36}{48}$$
$$= \frac{106}{48}$$

To change the improper fraction $\frac{106}{48}$ to a mixed number, divide 106 by 48.

$$48 \overline{)106} \quad \begin{array}{r} 2 \\ \end{array}$$
$$\begin{array}{r} -96 \\ \hline 10 \end{array}$$

The quotient of 2 is the whole number part, and the remainder of 10 goes over the divisor of 48 to show the additional fraction. They ate $2\frac{10}{48}$ or $2\frac{5}{24}$ pizzas.

OOOOOOOOOOOO

Sondra looked over the table. "After all that talk about how hungry we were, not one of us finished a pizza," she said sadly.

"Well, I did my best," Jennifer said, "but you left more than either of us did."

"Maybe we should have just gotten 2 pizzas," Taylor suggested, but Sondra shook her head.

"We ate more than 2, but we have a lot left over."

OOOOOOOOOOOO

How much pizza is left over? You could add up the amounts each of the kids left, but since you already added up how much they ate, it might be easier to just subtract $3 - 2\dfrac{5}{24}$. You can do that problem by changing to improper fractions or by regrouping.

If you use improper fractions, you want to translate 3 into a fraction. Since any whole number can be written as a fraction by giving it a denominator of 1, $3 = \dfrac{3}{1}$. Next, you need to change $2\dfrac{5}{24}$ back to an improper fraction. Multiply 24 times 2 and add that to the 5. $2\dfrac{5}{24} = \dfrac{24 \times 2 + 5}{24} = \dfrac{53}{24}$. Once you have both numbers as improper fractions, use the bow tie. You can use the bow tie for subtraction as well as addition. You do almost the same exact things.

First, multiply up from right to left and put the product over the left side. Then, multiply up from the left to the right and put the product over the right side. Then, multiply the denominators and put the product under the fraction bar as the new denominator. Now, for the different part: Instead of adding the two floating numbers, you subtract them! Not surprising, is it?

$$\frac{3}{1} - \frac{53}{24} = \frac{^{72}3}{1} - \frac{53^{53}}{_{24}24} = \frac{72-53}{24} = \frac{19}{24}$$

The combined leftovers make up $\dfrac{19}{24}$ of a pizza.

If you want to use regrouping to subtract, you imagine breaking up the 3 as 2 + 1 and then changing the 1 to $\dfrac{24}{24}$. $3 - 2\dfrac{5}{24} = 2\dfrac{24}{24} - 2\dfrac{5}{24} = \dfrac{19}{24}$.

FRACTIONS

1. What fractional part of the pie is shaded?

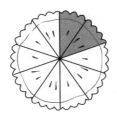

2. What fractional part of the pie is shaded? Put this fraction in its most reduced form.

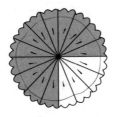

3. What fractional part of the pie is shaded? Combine it with the fraction of the pie in question 2 above, and then put this final fraction in its most reduced form.

4. $3\dfrac{1}{2} - 1\dfrac{2}{5} =$

5. $9\dfrac{2}{3} + 1\dfrac{1}{2} =$

6. Rose has $\dfrac{1}{4}$ of an apple pie, and her friend has $\dfrac{2}{4}$ of the same pie. Together, Rose and her friend have what fractional part of the apple pie?

7. Lionel has $\dfrac{1}{4}$ of a bag of candy, his generous sister gives him $\dfrac{1}{2}$ of a bag of candy, and his mother, who doesn't know how much candy he already has or she wouldn't give it to him, gives him $\dfrac{1}{4}$

of a bag of candy. What fractional part of a bag of candy does Lionel have at the end of all this giving? Reduce.

8. Sondra had $\dfrac{6}{7}$ of a chocolate cake, and then her sister took $\dfrac{2}{5}$ of Sondra's part of the cake. What fractional part of the chocolate cake does Sondra have now, and do you think it is approximately more or less than $\dfrac{1}{2}$ of the cake?

9. Taylor had 3 complete checker sets and $\dfrac{2}{3}$ of another. Then his uncle gave him 4 whole checker sets and $\dfrac{5}{6}$ of another. How many checker sets did Taylor end up with? Try to approximate first.

10. Jennifer bought $10\dfrac{3}{4}$ gallons of fake blood to play some kind of terrible trick on her good friend Taylor. On her way to set up the trick, she spilled $3\dfrac{7}{8}$ gallons of fake blood. How much blood did she have left? Before you even start the problem, estimate whether she will have enough blood after the spill if she needs at least 6 gallons for the trick.

OOOOOOOOOOOO

"Quitting already?" Mr. Ippolitto asked with a smile. He glanced from Sondra to Jennifer to Taylor. "Shall I pack the rest up for you?"

"May...be..." Jennifer stretched the word out. "Maybe I could manage another half a piece," she said.

"You can't be serious," Taylor said, as Jennifer reached for the pizza cutter.

Jennifer cut one of her remaining slices into 2 pieces.

OOOOOOOOOOOO

Another way to say this is that Jennifer was taking $\frac{1}{2}$ of $\frac{1}{6}$. Almost any time you see the word "of" in a math problem, it means that you should multiply.

Multiplying fractions is easier than adding or subtracting them. To multiply fractions, you just multiply the top and the bottom straight across. No common denominator is needed! So $\frac{1}{2}$ of $\frac{1}{6}$ becomes $\frac{1}{12}$. The 1 times 1 of the numerators becomes 1, and the 2 times 6 of the denominators becomes 12.

This "of" trick works even if 1 of the numbers isn't a fraction. For example, what is $\frac{1}{4}$ of 12? To multiply a fraction by a whole number, it is usually easier to look at the whole number as a fraction. Any whole number can be expressed as a fraction, if it is put over 1. Then multiply straight across and reduce. $\frac{1}{4} \times \frac{12}{1} = \frac{12}{4} = \frac{3}{1} = 3$.

A great thing about multiplying is that you have access to an extremely cool tool: cancellation. Cancellation is a bit like reducing the fractions before you multiply them. To cancel, you try to find common factors in the diagonal parts of the 2 fractions being multiplied.

Look at the problem $\frac{2}{3} \times \frac{9}{16}$, and look especially at the numbers diagonally across from one another. Do 3 and 9 have any common factors? Sure, 3 is a factor of both of them. So divide both by 3 and cancel the numbers.

$$\frac{2}{\cancel{3}_1} \times \frac{\cancel{9}^3}{16}$$

Look at the other diagonal. Do 2 and 16 have any common factors? Sure, 2 is a factor of both of them. Divide by 2 and cancel the numbers.

$$\frac{\cancel{2}^1}{\cancel{3}_1} \times \frac{\cancel{9}^3}{\cancel{16}_8}$$

Now multiply straight across.

$$\frac{\cancel{2}^1}{\cancel{3}_1} \times \frac{\cancel{9}^3}{\cancel{16}_8} = \frac{1 \times 3}{1 \times 8} = \frac{3}{8}$$

Of course, it would have worked without cancellation, but then you would have had to reduce at the end.

To multiply mixed numbers, translate them into improper fractions. $3\frac{1}{2} \times 2\frac{1}{5}$ becomes $\frac{7}{2} \times \frac{11}{5} = \frac{77}{10} = 7\frac{7}{10}$.

⬭⬭⬭⬭⬭⬭⬭⬭⬭⬭⬭⬭

Mr. Ippolitto watched with amusement, and Sondra and Taylor watched with amazement, as Jennifer ate just a little more pizza. Finally, she declared herself finished.

"Do you each want your own box," Mr. Ippolitto asked, "or should I put it all into 1 box for you to share later?"

"If each of us has our own box, it will be easier to take home," Taylor suggested.

"Maybe," said Jennifer, "but it seems wasteful to use 3 boxes for what will fit in 1."

"How would we share it?" Sondra wondered aloud. "The pieces are all different sizes. It would be hard to divide it up fairly."

OOOOOOOOOOO

A little while ago, we calculated that the combined leftovers make up $\frac{19}{24}$ of a pizza, but then Jennifer ate another half of 1 of her slices, or another $\frac{1}{12}$ of a pizza. That means that now they have $\frac{19}{24} - \frac{1}{12}$ of a pizza left over. $\frac{19}{24} - \frac{1}{12} = \frac{19}{24} - \frac{2}{24} = \frac{17}{24}$, so the leftovers make up $\frac{17}{24}$ of a pizza.

If you think about sharing the pizza as giving each of the 3 kids an equal number of pieces, you will see why Sondra thinks it will be difficult. If you imagine the pizza cut into tiny slices so that each slice is $\frac{1}{24}$ of the pizza, you can see that 17 of them can't be equally shared by 3 kids. Because dividing 17 by 3 leaves a remainder of 2, it is not possible to share 17 of anything equally among 3 people. Each person would get 5 of those tiny slices, or $\frac{5}{24}$, but there would be another $\frac{2}{24}$ or $\frac{1}{12}$ left over.

But is there any way to divide the leftover $\frac{17}{24}$ of a pizza among the kids? Another way to ask that question is to ask what you get if you divide $\frac{17}{24}$ by 3. Whenever you are trying to figure out how many pieces something can be split into, you are dealing with a division problem. How does one divide a fraction?

To divide by a fraction, invert the dividing fraction (flip it) and multiply. Invert means turn upside down, so $\frac{1}{16}$ would become $\frac{16}{1}$, and $\frac{2}{1}$ would become $\frac{1}{2}$. The new fraction formed when a fraction is inverted is called the reciprocal (just a fancy word for a flipped fraction). So $\frac{1}{3}$ is the reciprocal of 3 or $\frac{3}{1}$.

So, if $\frac{17}{24}$ of a pizza is divided among 3 kids, you would divide by 3, which means multiplying by $\frac{1}{3}$.

$$\frac{17}{24} \div \frac{3}{1} = \frac{17}{24} \times \frac{1}{3} = \frac{17}{72}$$

Even Sondra wouldn't have the patience to cut the pizza into 72 pieces, so that answer isn't much help. Most people would think that $\frac{1}{8}$ of a pizza is a typical slice, so you could ask a different question. How many slices, each $\frac{1}{8}$ of a pizza, are in $\frac{17}{24}$? Answering that question means dividing $\frac{17}{24}$ by $\frac{1}{8}$.

$$\frac{17}{24} \div \frac{1}{8} = \frac{17}{24} \times \frac{8}{1}$$

Here's a place to use cancellation. Since the problem above is now a multiplication problem, you can cancel if you want to. However, never ever cancel when you have a division problem set up. Only cancel when you have a multiplication problem set up.

$$\frac{17}{24} \div \frac{1}{8} = \frac{17}{\underset{3}{24}} \times \frac{\overset{1}{8}}{1} = \frac{17}{3} = 5\frac{2}{3}$$

Well, that means that you could make 5 slices that are each an eighth of a pizza, and then there would be $\frac{2}{3}$ of a slice left. That will still be hard to share.

Of course, this division strategy works with mixed numbers, too. All you do is convert them to improper fractions before you start.

$$4\frac{1}{2} \div 2\frac{2}{3} = \frac{2 \times 4 + 1}{2} \div \frac{3 \times 2 + 2}{3}$$
$$= \frac{9}{2} \div \frac{8}{3}$$
$$= \frac{9}{2} \times \frac{3}{8}$$
$$= \frac{27}{16}$$
$$= 1\frac{11}{16}$$

Have you figured out why you invert the fraction? Well, if you were going to divide 6 kids into 2 groups, how would you do it? You would divide 6 by 2. That can look like this: $6 \div 2$ or $\frac{6}{2}$. Look at that last one. Six over

2 is the same thing as $6 \times \frac{1}{2}$. So to divide by 2, you actually multiply by $\frac{1}{2}$. Every time you divide, you are merely multiplying by the number's reciprocal!

MULTIPLYING AND DIVIDING FRACTIONS

1. $\frac{1}{2} \times \frac{1}{3} =$

2. $\frac{2}{5} \times \frac{1}{9} =$

3. $\frac{1}{2} \div \frac{1}{2} =$

4. $3\frac{1}{2} \times \frac{2}{3} =$

5. $3\frac{1}{3} \div 5\frac{2}{9} =$

6. Taylor has 6 bags of marbles. If he wants to give away $\frac{4}{5}$ of them, how many bags will he give away? (Put your answer in the form of a mixed number. It will be easier to understand that way.)

7. Sondra has $\frac{7}{8}$ of a pizza. How many skinny little $\frac{1}{32}$-sized slices are there in her $\frac{7}{8}$?

8. Taylor has $\frac{1}{5}$ of an apple and he wants to give his brother $\frac{1}{3}$ of it. How much of the apple is Taylor going to give his brother?

9. Taylor and Jennifer have $3\frac{1}{2}$ cantaloupes. Jennifer is going on a picnic and she wants to take $\frac{1}{5}$ of their cantaloupe stash with her. How much cantaloupe will she take? Will it even be 1 whole cantaloupe? Can you approximate before you do the problem?

10. Jennifer has a bug collection that consists of $5\frac{3}{5}$ bags of bugs. How many $\frac{1}{4}$-bags of bugs does she have in her collection?

OOOOOOOOOOO

After some discussion, Taylor, Jennifer and Sondra agreed to pack the leftover pizza in 1 box, although they could not find an easy solution for sharing it. Jennifer offered to try to eat a little more to make the leftovers easier to divide, but everyone agreed that overeating was not a good idea, especially on such a hot day.

"Well, then," Mr. Ippolitto said, "I'll pack this up for you." He gathered up their plates and took a few steps away from the table before he stopped and looked back at them. "Wait. You're not going home now, are you?" The 3 kids all shook their heads. "Well, then, you don't want to carry this box around all afternoon. How about I leave it in the refrigerator in the storeroom, and you can pick it up later? You still remember the access code?"

They assured him that they did remember, thanked him again, and finished their lemonade while Mr. Ippolitto packed their leftover pizza into a box and placed it in the storeroom refrigerator.

REVIEW

1. Which two of the following 5 numbers are equal?

$$\frac{1}{5} \quad \frac{3}{6} \quad \frac{2}{3} \quad \frac{1}{2} \quad \frac{4}{10}$$

2. $\dfrac{1}{2} + \dfrac{1}{3} =$

3. $\dfrac{3}{4} \div \dfrac{2}{3} =$

4. $\dfrac{3}{8} \times 3\dfrac{2}{3} =$

5. $3\dfrac{1}{2} \div 5\dfrac{1}{2}$

6. Rose has $\dfrac{2}{3}$ of a pizza pie. Is that the same as if she had $\dfrac{3}{6}$ of a pizza pie?

7. Taylor has $\dfrac{1}{2}$ of a box of dominoes. Taylor's friend says, "I want $\dfrac{1}{3}$ of those dominoes." If Taylor gives his friend what he asks for, what part of the box of dominoes will Taylor give away?

8. Sondra has $3\frac{3}{8}$ gallons of glue. If fixing a certain statue only uses $\frac{1}{4}$ of the glue, how much glue will the repair use? And how much glue will she have left?

9. Taylor has $2\frac{2}{3}$ buckets of nails, but the nails are very heavy, so he wants to put them into buckets that are filled up only $\frac{1}{4}$ of the way. How many $\frac{1}{4}$-full buckets could he separate his nails into?

10. Jennifer has $5\frac{3}{4}$ bags of hair. If she was able to sell $\frac{3}{8}$ of the hair to a farmer to scare away deer, how much of the hair is she left with?

⊙⊙⊙⊙⊙⊙⊙⊙⊙⊙⊙⊙

Terrific! You are officially a fraction superstar. So let's go onward and upward to the next math challenge!

CHAPTER 4

Decimals

"Are you folks ready for your check?" the woman behind the counter inquired. Taylor, Jennifer, and Sondra looked at one another, remembering their earlier estimate of their cash—or lack of it. The woman turned away to speak to another customer before they had a chance to answer.

"Uh, that was a great lunch," Taylor said, "but how are we going to pay for it? We are seriously short of money, remember?"

"Well, Mr. Ippolitto said he'd pay us for moving the boxes," Jennifer reminded him.

Taylor started to nod, then switched direction, and shook his head. "Do you know how much that will be?" he asked.

The girls were silent for a moment, and then Sondra spoke up. "Let's see if we can get an estimate." She looked at a menu. "They're $6.95 each, and lemonade is $2.50 per pitcher."

"Yikes! Didn't we say we only had about 7 dollars?" Jennifer asked.

"$7.26," Sondra replied. "That would pay for 1 pizza. So, we need enough for 2 pizzas and 2 pitchers of lemonade. Did we earn about $19.00?"

| 6.95 | 2.50 | 7.26 |

Do you recognize these types of numbers? Sure, because almost all monetary amounts are written out this way. These numbers are called decimals. Decimals are another type of fraction.

Sondra has 5 dollars and 23 cents; this is written in number form as 5.23. (We're leaving out the dollar sign because the things we're writing about apply to all numbers written in this form, not just American money.) The whole in this case is a dollar. Sondra has 5 whole dollars, and 0.23 parts of another dollar. What is another way of looking at 0.23? $\frac{23}{100}$ Did you ever think about why pennies are called cents? The root "cent" is part of the word century and centennial. It means 100. There are 100 cents in a dollar, so each cent, or penny, is $\frac{1}{100}$ of a dollar. And 23 cents are $\frac{23}{100}$ of a dollar.

THINK ABOUT THIS

Decimals that don't have whole numbers—for example, if you have only cents and no whole dollars—are almost always written with a 0 in the ones place. Why? It helps to show where the decimal point is. The important thing about decimals is the decimal point. The decimal point is the dot to the right of the units digit.

$$5.23$$

Do you remember place values? Well, there are even more places for digits than you might have thought. The place directly to the right of the decimal point is called the tenths place.

$$5.23$$
↑
tenth

This shows two-tenths, or $\frac{2}{10}$. That's why we have dimes; dimes are tenths of dollars. To the right of the tenths place is the hundredths place.

$$5.23$$
$$\uparrow$$

hundredth

This shows there are 3 one-hundredths, or $\frac{3}{100}$, better known in dollar form as 3 cents. Altogether, it is 23 one hundredths, better known as 23 cents.

To read the whole number aloud as a decimal, say "five and twenty three hundredths" or "five point two three."

How did Jennifer approximate those numbers? She used a method to make approximating easier, called rounding. When you round, you take numbers and get rid of their smaller, less important parts. If you were a big business executive and wanted to buy a building, you probably wouldn't say it cost 5 million, 10 dollars and 14 cents. The 10 dollars and 14 cents would get rounded off, and you would say, "This building costs about 5 million dollars."

Here is how to round. First, find out to what digit place you are rounding. Suppose you wanted to round to the tens place. We will round 234 to the tens place. Notice that it's "tens," not "tenths." Here is the tens place of a number.

$$234$$
$$\uparrow$$

tens

Start from the place to which you are rounding, which we'll call the key place, and look at the digit directly to the right. If that digit is 5 or more, add 1 to the digit in the key place. If that digit is less than 5, leave the digit in the key place as it is. Replace all the digits to the right of the key place with zeros.

For example, try rounding 234 to the tens place. The digit to the right of the tens place is 4. Is 4 larger or smaller than 5? Smaller, so the digit in the tens place, 3, will stay the same. 234 becomes 230.

Take a look at a number line.

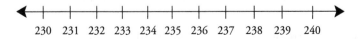

Is 234 closer to 230 or 240? The number line shows you that 234 is closer to 230.

Try another example. Round 3,761 to the hundreds place. Which digit is in the hundreds place? It's the 7. First, look at the digit to the right of the 7. It is larger than 5, so the 7 becomes an 8. Then, all the digits to the right, the 6 and the 1, turn to zeros. 3,761 becomes 3,800.

To see this more clearly, look at a number line.

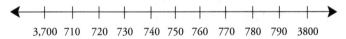

Which hundred is 3,761 closer to: 3,800 or the 3,700? The number line is a great way to see how rounding works.

Decimals round the same way. Try rounding 34.12 to the tenths place. The tenths place is just to the right of the decimal point, where the 1 is. The digit to the right of the tens place is 2. Is 2 greater or less than 5? Less, so the 1 stays the same and the digit to the right of it turn to 0. 34.12 becomes 34.10 (or 34.1). The decimal isn't affected by the 0 at the end the way a whole number would be.

THINK ABOUT THIS

A 0 at the end of a decimal doesn't affect that decimal's value. Why?

Think about how decimals look when they are fractions. 0.5 is really $\frac{5}{10}$ and 0.50 is really $\frac{50}{100}$. Can you reduce these? $\frac{5}{10} \div \frac{5}{5} = \frac{1}{2}$ and $\frac{50}{100} \div \frac{10}{10} = \frac{5}{10} \div \frac{5}{5} = \frac{1}{2}$. Even reduced, they are the same number. You could add 10 trillion zeroes to the right of a decimal, and it wouldn't make a speck of difference.

A peculiar thing can happen if the digit in the key place is a 9. Round the number 45.97 to the nearest tenth. The digit in the tenths place is a 9, and the digit to the right of it is a 7. Since 7 is more than 5, you want to increase the digit in the tenths place by 1, but that makes the 9 turn into a 10, and you can't fit a 10 in the place of a single digit. Think about what the numbers are saying. They're telling you that you have 10 tenths, and 10 tenths make 1 whole. 45.97 rounds up to 45 and 10 tenths, or 45 and 1 whole—otherwise known as 46.0.

As a shortcut, remember that when the digit in the key place starts out as a 9 and needs to round up to 10, put the 0 in the key place, and carry the 1 over to the next place to the left. Try rounding 73.498 to the nearest hundredth. There's a 9 in the hundredths place and an 8 in the next place to the right. That means you round up, which changes the 9 to 10. Put a 0 in the hundredths place and carry the 1 to the tenths place.

$$73.498 \Rightarrow 73.4\overset{10}{\_}0 \Rightarrow 73.\overset{4+1}{\_}00 \Rightarrow 73.500 \cdot$$

Jennifer and Taylor barely had time to admit they didn't know how much they had earned when the woman from the counter brought over their check and dropped it on the table. Taylor thought it was odd that she said "thank you" since they hadn't given her anything yet.

"It should be about $26," Sondra warned, as Taylor reluctantly turned the paper over.

$$\begin{array}{r} \$6.95 \\ \$6.95 \\ \$6.95 \\ + \ \underline{\$5.00} \\ \$25.85 \end{array}$$

$$\bullet\bullet\bullet\bullet\bullet\bullet\bullet\bullet\bullet\bullet\bullet\bullet$$

How did Sondra calculate that the check was about 26 dollars? She added rounded decimals. Since decimals are another type of fraction, the way to add them will not surprise you: You need a common denominator. What may surprise you is that a common denominator for decimals only means line up the decimals according to their places.

This: $\begin{array}{r} 2.3 \\ + \ \underline{3.} \end{array}$ Not this: $+ \ \cancel{\begin{array}{r} 2.3 \\ 3. \end{array}}$

Can you figure out how this works? Well, what would the denominators of all the numbers in the hundredths place be if they were fractions? That's right, hundredths means denominators of 100. And the tenths place has denominators of 10. Decimals can even go further to the right, to the thousandths place and beyond.

$$0.052$$
$$\uparrow$$

thousandths

When these numbers are lined up, everything in the same decimal place has the same denominator, and you can just add.

Try it with the rounded numbers that Jennifer added.

$$\begin{array}{rcl}
\$6.95 & \Rightarrow & 7.00 \\
\$6.95 & \Rightarrow & 7.00 \\
\$6.95 & \Rightarrow & 7.00 \\
+\ \underline{\$5.00} & \Rightarrow & \underline{5.00} \\
\$25.85 & & 26.00
\end{array}$$

Rounding worked pretty well as an approximating tool, didn't it?

"Hold on, just a minute," Mr. Ippolitto called. He walked over to the table and took the check from Taylor's hand. "No, this isn't right," he said, pulling a pen from his apron pocket. He looked around as though he had lost something, then he sat down in the fourth chair at the table. "First of all, moving boxes is thirsty work, especially in this heat. The first pitcher of lemonade is on me." He made wrote a few numbers on the check and did some arithmetic. Jennifer looked over his shoulder and saw this adjustment.

$$\begin{array}{r}
\$25.85 \\
-\underline{\$2.50} \\
\$23.35
\end{array}$$

Subtracting decimals works the same way as adding. Just line up the decimal places and subtract as you would any number.

$$\begin{array}{r} 3.05 \\ -2.2 \\ \hline \end{array} \quad \text{becomes} \quad \begin{array}{r} {}^{2}\cancel{3}.{}^{1}05 \\ -\ 2.20 \\ \hline 0.85 \end{array}$$

As you can see here, if you have a number without a digit in one of the decimal places, you can just add a 0 to make it less confusing. This is most helpful when you subtract.

QUIZ #5

DECIMALS

1. Round 234 to the nearest hundred.

2. Round 13.45 to the nearest tenth.

3. Round 2.34 and 3.45 to the nearest tenth, and then add the 2 rounded numbers.

4. $10.879 - 7.345 =$

5. $12.3 + 7.52 =$

6. Sondra has 2 dollars and 32 cents. Which digit occupies the tenths place (if written as a dollar amount)?

7. Taylor has 3 dollars and 79 cents, and he washes his uncle's car and earns 2 dollars and 50 cents. How much money does Taylor have at the end?

8. Sondra has 2 dollars and 32 cents and gives away 1 dollar and 98 cents. How much money does she have left? Express it as a fractional part of 1 dollar.

9. Taylor has 2.3537 grams of gold and is going to buy 0.0023 more grams tomorrow. How much gold will he have tomorrow after his purchase?

10. Jennifer had 4.3 gallons of cement and used 2.78 gallons to build a small fortress (very small). How much cement does she have left?

○○○○○○○○○○○○

"Now, of course, we can't forget to calculate your earnings," Mr. Ippolitto said. "Loading the storeroom took you an hour and 15 minutes. Let's write that as 1.25 hours. That's a total of 3.75 hours of work."

○○○○○○○○○○○○

How did 1 hour and 15 minutes turn into 1.25 hours? The 1 whole hour is the digit in the ones place. There are 60 minutes in an hour, so 15 minutes is $\frac{15}{60} = \frac{1}{4}$ of an hour, and $\frac{1}{4} = \frac{25}{100} = 0.25$. So 1 hour and 15 minutes is $1\frac{1}{4}$ hours or 1.25 hours.

THINK ABOUT THIS

You already know that to multiply a number by 10 or a power of 10, you add a 0 onto that number. For instance, $3 \times 10 = 30$. What you are actually doing is moving the decimal point to the right. $3.0 \times 10 = 30$. When you divide by a power of 10, move the decimal point to the left. For example, let's say you wanted to divide 3,000 by 10. $3000 \div 10 = 300.0$

A decimal like 1.25 can be rewritten in many different ways. To help you understand the rules for multiplying decimals, we're going to write it as $125 \div 100$. When Mr. Ippolitto multiplied 3 times 1.25, he was multiplying $3 \times 125 \div 100$. $3 \times 125 = 375$ so that problem becomes $375 \div 100$ or 3.75.

To multiply decimals, simply set up an ordinary multiplication problem. You don't have to align the decimal point as you do with addition or subtraction. Just multiply as though the decimal point wasn't even there. Next, count the number of decimal places in the numbers you multiplied. In this case, there are 2 spaces to the right of the decimal point in 1.25 and none in 3, so you need to place the decimal point 2 places left of the end. Start at the right of 375, and count over 2 decimal places to the left. 375 becomes 3.75.

$$
\begin{array}{rcl}
1.25 & \Rightarrow & 125 \div 100 \\
\times\ 3 & \Rightarrow & \times\ 3 \\
\hline
3.75 & \Rightarrow & 375 \div 100
\end{array}
$$

○○○○○○○○○○○

"I promised you minimum wage. Do you kids know how much that is?"

Taylor, Jennifer and Sondra exchanged shrugs. "I thought you just meant you were going to pay us as little as possible," Jennifer admitted.

Mr. Ippolitto laughed. "Well, you're all still a bit too young for real jobs, but minimum wage is $6.75 per hour, so we'll calculate using that."

Taylor tried to estimate. "You mean we earned about 7 dollars?"

"Your estimate is a little low," Mr. Ippolitto said. "Remember you worked more than an hour. You each earned more than 8 dollars."

OOOOOOOOOOOOO

Multiplying a decimal times a decimal isn't very different from multiplying a decimal by a whole number. Multiplying 6.75×1.25 is like multiplying 675×125 and then adjusting the decimal point. $675 \times 125 = 84375$, and you can use estimation to guess where the decimal point might go. 6.75 is about 7 and 1.25 is about 1, so the answer, as Taylor guessed, would be about 7. That means it's likely to be 8.4375, rather than 84.375 or 843.75.

$$
\begin{array}{l}
6.75 \Rightarrow 675 \div 100 \\
1.25 \Rightarrow 125 \div 100
\end{array} \bigg| \begin{array}{l} \text{Multiply 675 by 125} \\ \text{and remember the two "} \div 100 \text{" for later} \end{array}
$$

$$
\begin{array}{r}
3375 \\
1350 \\
675 \\
\hline
84375
\end{array}
$$

$84375 \underbrace{\div 100 \div 100}_{\text{Now think about these}} = 843.75 \div 100 = 8.4375$

When you multiply decimals by other decimals, multiply the numbers as if there were no decimals, then count up the number of places to the right of the decimal point in both numbers. Use that total to place the decimal point in the answer. Count from the end of the answer, and go that many places left. There are 2 decimal places in 1.25 and 2 decimal places in 6.75, so the answer will have 4 decimal places. Start at the right of the 5 in 84375 and move the decimal four places left: 8.4375.

Now, a number like 8.4375 doesn't make much sense if you're talking about dollars and cents. You have 8 dollars, 4 dimes (for the tenths place), and 3 pennies (for the hundredths place), but there are no coins for the thousandths place or the ten-thousandths place. Those extra places would actually represent fractions of a penny. At a time like this, you really need to round.

For dollars and cents, you want to round 8.4375 to the hundredths place. Right now, that's a 3. The digit to the right of that is a 7, which is more than 5, so add 1 to make the 3 into a 4, and replace the 7 and the 5 with zeros. You get 8.4375 = 8.4400. Now you can drop those trailing zeros and know that each of the kids earned $8.44.

○○○○○○○○○○○○

"So let's figure out your total earnings," Mr. Ippolitto said. He multiplied 4.75 times 6.75, and rounded his answer.

$$
\begin{array}{r}
6.75 \\
\times\ 4.75 \\
\hline
3375 \\
4725 \\
+\ 2700 \\
\hline
32.0625 \Rightarrow 32.06
\end{array}
$$

"The 3 of you together earned $32.06. That will more than cover your lunch. Let's see how much I still owe you." He subtracted 23.25 from 32.06.

$$
\begin{array}{r}
3\,^1\!\!\not{2}.\,^1 06 \\
2\ \ 3.25 \\
\hline
8.81
\end{array}
$$

"OK, I owe you an additional $8.81."

○○○○○○○○○○○○

Now let's say, excited by the money they were making, the kids decided to split up their income 3 ways. How would you figure this out? You could do it by dividing 8.81 by 3. Here is how the division problem would look.

$$3\overline{)8.81}$$

To divide a decimal by a whole number, simply let the decimal point float straight up. Then divide as you normally would, leaving the decimal point where it is.

$$
\begin{array}{r}
2.93 \\
3\overline{)8.81} \\
-\ 6 \\
\hline
28 \\
-\ 27 \\
\hline
11 \\
-\ 9 \\
\hline
2
\end{array}
$$

How about dividing decimals by other decimals? You don't. Really, you never divide by a decimal. Instead, you come up with an equivalent problem, one that has the same answer, but has a whole number as its divisor. Divide, for example, 2.5 by 0.5. Try thinking about this division problem written as a fraction: $\dfrac{2.5}{0.5}$. Now you want to multiply by a disguised 1 to change the denominator to a whole number. You want to move the decimal point 1 place, so multiply by $\dfrac{10}{10}$.

$$
\frac{2.5}{0.5} \times \frac{10}{10} = \frac{25}{5}
$$

When you see it that way, the answer is easy, isn't it? Here's how it looks in a more traditional division setup. $0.5\overline{)2.5}$ Move the decimal point in the divisor, in this case 0.5, over to the right until it is a whole number. In this case, that means moving the decimal point one space to the right. Then you must move the decimal point in the dividend, the 2.5, over the same number of spaces. In this case, move the decimal point 1 space to the right. Then divide normally and let the decimal point float up.

$$0.5\overline{)2.5.}^{\displaystyle 5.}$$

Try another one. Divide 14.375 by 2.25. To change 2.25 to a whole number, you need to move the decimal point 2 places to the right, so move the decimal point in 14.375 2 places right as well. Now your division problem is 1437.5 divided by 225.

```
              6.3
    2.25.)14.37.5
        −  1350
           ─────
            875
        −   675
           ─────
            200
```

If you wish, you can add one or more zeros to the end of the dividend, and continue dividing. (Whether you want to or not will depend on the question you're trying to answer.) Here's what the problem looks like if we add a few zeros.

```
              6.388
    2.25.)14.37.500
        −  1350
           ─────
            875
        −   675
           ─────
           2000
        −  1800
           ─────
           2000
        −  1800
           ─────
            200
```

What if you divide a whole number by a decimal? Well, you still move the decimal point. Whole numbers have decimal points, but they just aren't usually visible. In a whole number, the decimal point is at the end, and you can add zeros after the decimal point.

$$.05\overline{)30} \Rightarrow .05\overline{)30.00} \Rightarrow .05.\overline{)30.00.} \Rightarrow 5\overline{)3000}$$

THINK ABOUT THIS

Sometimes it is much simpler to set decimal division up as fractions first. For instance, $0.57 \div 0.01$ may look confusing, but you can set it up first as a fraction, $\dfrac{0.57}{0.01}$. Move the decimal points in both the numerator and the denominator the same number of places. Thus, $0.57 \div 0.01$ is actually $\dfrac{0.57}{0.01} \times \dfrac{100}{100} = \dfrac{57}{1}$, and you know that any number divided by 1 is still the same number. Therefore, $0.57 \div 0.01$ is simply equal to 57. Cool, huh?

YET ANOTHER THING TO THINK ABOUT

When dividing by decimals such as 0.01, you can use the same shortcut you use when multiplying by tens. To divide by 0.01 is to divide by $\dfrac{1}{100}$, which means to multiply by 100, which means to move the decimal point two places to the right. You don't always have to think of it exactly this way, but it is nice to know that the connection is there, isn't it?

MULTIPLYING AND DIVIDING DECIMALS

1. $2.3 \times 4 =$

2. $3.4 \div 2 =$

3. $2.1 \times 3.2 =$

4. $1.8 \div 0.9 =$

5. $2.3 \div 0.01 =$

6. If Taylor gets 3 dollars and 40 cents every time he empties his piggy bank, how much money will he have after he empties his piggy bank four times?

7. If Taylor has 5.2 ounces of orange juice in a glass and he separates it into 2 glasses that hold equal amounts, how many ounces of orange juice will each of the 2 glasses hold?

8. Taylor and Jennifer together have 7 dollars and they want to divide it into groups of 50 cents each. How many groups of 50 cents each would they have?

9. Jennifer receives 3.02 pounds of gelatin every time she knocks out the clown in the neighborhood carnival. If she knocks the clown out 2.5 times on an average day, how many pounds of gelatin does she get on an average day? How many pounds does she get if you approximate first?

10. Jennifer has 0.45 ounces of milk in a glass, and she wants to separate it into glasses that each hold 0.05 ounces of milk. How

many of these teeny-tiny glasses will she need? How many do you approximate she will need?

You can also look at regular-old division as decimals. For instance, $\frac{5}{10}$ is not only $\frac{1}{2}$, but also $5 \div 10$. Remember, the fraction bar means divide. Put the decimal place on top of the roof and you have $10\overline{)5} \Rightarrow 10\overline{)5.0}^{\,0.5}$

REVIEW

1. $2.3 + 4 =$

2. $3.5 - 2.7 =$

3. $1.2 \times 4 =$

4. $3.2 \div 2 =$

5. $2.4 \div 0.6 =$

6. Jennifer has 45 cents and she gets 2 dollars and 55 cents for her birthday. How much money does she have altogether?

7. Taylor had 3 dollars and 15 cents and spent 1 dollar and 27 cents on a new box of tissues. How much is he left with?

8. For each basket Sondra makes at a charity basketball game, Barbara the bike-store owner donates 35 cents to the charity. If

Sondra makes 6 baskets, how much money will Barbara donate to the charity? Can you approximate first?

9. Taylor receives 2.3 grams of silver every time he does a favor for his science teacher. If he does 5 favors, how many grams of silver will he receive? Express your answer as a mixed number.

10. Jennifer wants to divide her 6.35 ounces of feathers into piles containing 0.5 ounces of feathers each. How many piles will there be at the end of the separation?

Terrific. Now keep going forward to see where decimals can lead you.

CHAPTER 5

Ratio and Percentages

The sun was still high when Sondra, Taylor, and Jennifer found themselves back on the sidewalk outside Mr. Ippolitto's shop. The center of town had little in the way of shade or breeze, so they returned to the familiar problem.

"It's hot," Taylor said, stating the obvious.

"Do we have enough money to go to the movies?" Jennifer asked. Sondra made a quick estimate. "We could have managed the first show if we skipped the concession stand, but we won't make the full price admission."

"Why do we have to pay full price?" Taylor whined. "Couldn't we negotiate? What if we just tell them how much we want to pay and see if they'll take it?"

"That's it! Sondra exclaimed. She started walking toward the town center. "You're brilliant!" she called back to Taylor.

"Where are we going?" Jennifer asked.

"The museum," Sondra explained. "They have a pay-what-you-wish policy," she explained, "and it's air-conditioned."

It took a moment for their eyes to adjust to the filtered light in the main hall of the museum. The marble walls and floors reinforced the sensation of coolness that the air-conditioning created. Jennifer tilted her head back to look up at the ceiling 30 feet above them and turned in slow circles until she started to get dizzy.

"Well, we're here," Taylor said, "so what do we do now?"

"That looks interesting," Jennifer said, pointing to a banner over the central corridor. The 3 kids moved down the corridor toward what the banner described as Secrets of the City. When the hallway widened into a room, they were amazed by what they saw. Spread out on a platform in the center of the exhibit hall, enclosed in protective glass, was a perfect model of the city. Observation decks at different places around the room let visitors view the miniature city from different levels. One especially high platform, described as the helicopter view, allowed them to see the entire city at once, as though they were flying overhead.

"Look! There's my house," Taylor exclaimed. The kids were able to locate the tiny models that represented each of their houses, their school, Mr. Ippolitto's restaurant, and the museum itself.

"How did they do this?" Jennifer wondered aloud. "How did they get everything just right—in the right place and just the right size?"

Taylor studied a sign on the glass enclosing the model. "It says it was built using a scale of 1 inch = 20 feet."

○○○○○○○○○○○

When you build a model, whether it's smaller than the original or bigger than the original, you are dealing with a **ratio**. Ratios are a way of comparing by dividing. The scale of the city model—1 inch to 20 feet—is a ratio. You can express the ratio of the miniature to the original as 1 : 20, as $\frac{1}{20}$, or as 1 to 20. All of these are said out loud as, "One-to-twenty."

In a ratio, the measurement units may or not be the same, so it's important to read carefully. The museum model uses different units—inches and feet—but you could change the 20 feet to 240 inches, and then the ratio, with the same units, would be 1 : 240. (Did you remember that there are 12 inches in a foot? You can think of that as a ratio too: 12 inches to 1 foot.) A ratio of 1 : 240 tells you that the actual city is 240 times the size of the model, or that a house that is really 20 feet tall is represented by a building 1 inch tall.

These ratios let you compare the sizes of the model and the real object, and that comparison is a multiplication or division style comparison. One object is so many times larger than the other is, or the smaller one is a certain fraction of the size of the other.

Now, you may be thinking that a ratio sounds a lot like a fraction, and you'd be right. Ratios and fractions are ways of comparing two numbers by dividing one by the other. The word ratio can be used to describe any comparison, but often that comparison is part to part, $\frac{part}{part}$, or small to large, $\frac{small}{large}$. If you make lemonade with 1 part sugar syrup to 3 parts lemon juice, the ratio of syrup to lemon juice would be 1 : 3, or $\frac{1}{3}$. The museum model makes things 1 inch long if they are 20 feet long in real life, so the ratio is 1 inch: 20 feet. The word fraction is used to mean a comparison of part to whole, $\frac{part}{whole}$, like eating 3 pieces of a pizza that was cut into 8 pieces. If you have a ratio of part to part, to get the whole you have to add up the parts. The lemonade with 1 part sugar syrup to 3 parts lemon juice has 4 parts altogether, so the lemon juice is 3 parts out of 4, or $\frac{3}{4}$.

When a ratio is used to compare parts, it often includes more than 2 numbers. This is called an **extended ratio**. If your lemonade were made with 1 part sugar syrup, 3 parts lemon juice and 5 parts water, you would write the extended ratio 1 : 3 : 5. That would make a total of 1 + 3 + 5 = 9 parts.

Keep an eye on the order of the parts in ratios. If you want the ratio of syrup to lemon juice, it is 1 : 3, but the ratio of lemon juice to syrup is 3 : 1. Stay on your toes and keep an eye out for which part comes first.

Ratios can be reduced, just like fractions. Ratios tell you what relative amounts are in a mixture. So, whether you make 1 million gallons of lemonade or just one glass, the ratio stays the same. For instance, if you are making fruit punch and you have a ratio of 4 parts grape juice to 6 parts apple juice in punch, you can reduce the ratio as if it were a fraction, changing 4 : 6, or $\frac{4}{6}$, to 2 : 3 or $\frac{2}{3}$. The ratio of 2 to 3 is the same as the ratio of 4 to 6, because for every 2 parts of grape juice there will always be 3 parts of apple juice. If the ratio is 2 to 3, it will always be 2 to 3, for a total of 5 parts. If you have 5 gallons of punch, it will be 2 gallons of grape juice and 3 gallons of apple juice. Whether you have 5 teeny-tiny cups of punch, or 5 million tanker trucks full of punch, the ratio will always be 2 parts grape juice to 3 parts apple juice.

Jennifer continued to stare at the model of the city, her eyes locked on the tiny representation of her house. "If that little thing is my house, what would a model of me look like?" she wondered.

Sondra straightened up from where she had been bending over the model and turned to look at Jennifer. After a moment, she looked back at the model, then at Jennifer, and back to the model again, and started to giggle.

"Don't laugh at me," Jennifer ordered.

"I can't help it," Sondra said. "You've always been the tallest one in our class. The idea of a teeny-tiny you is hysterical."

Taylor laughed out loud, then clamped his hand over his mouth when people turned to look at him. "If Jennifer is teeny-tiny, how big would you be?" he asked Sondra.

OOOOOOOOOOOO

How big would Sondra—or the model of Sondra—actually be? You know that the model of the city was built using the scale, or ratio, 1 inch to 20 feet. If Sondra were 20 feet tall in real life, the model of Sondra would be 1 inch tall, but Sondra is not even close to 20 feet tall.

Suppose Sondra is 5 feet tall. One way to figure out how big to make the model of Sondra is to realize that 5 feet is $\frac{1}{4}$ of 20 feet, so the model of Sondra should be $\frac{1}{4}$ of 1 inch, or $\frac{1}{4}$ inch tall. It's OK if the numbers work out nicely, but what if you wanted to make a model of Jennifer, who is 5 $\frac{1}{2}$ feet tall, or of Taylor, who is 5 feet, 2 inches tall?

What you need here are equal ratios. To build a model of Sondra, you want a ratio that's equal to 1 inch: 20 feet, but uses 5 feet, and that's $\frac{1}{4}$ inch: 5 feet.

$$\frac{1 \text{ inch}}{20 \text{ feet}} = \frac{\frac{1}{4} \text{ inch}}{5 \text{ feet}}$$

To build a model of Jennifer, you'd need to find the number of inches that would make these ratios equal.

$$\frac{1 \text{ inch}}{20 \text{ feet}} = \frac{? \text{ inches}}{5\frac{1}{2} \text{ feet}}$$

Two equal ratios make a **proportion**. Anytime you have two equal fractions or two equal ratios you have a proportion. $\frac{1}{2} = \frac{4}{8}$ is a proportion, and so is 6 : 7 = 12:14. If we tried to tell you that $\frac{1}{3} = \frac{5}{21}$, you would know that's just not true. Those fractions are not equal. That statement is not a proportion. When you know three of the numbers and you are trying to find the last number that will make it a proportion, you are **solving a proportion**.

There are two ways to solve a proportion. The first is to use what you know about equal fractions. Remember the punch that was made according to the ratio 2 parts of grape juice to 3 parts of apple juice? Suppose you wanted to make that punch, and you had 12 ounces of grape juice. How much apple juice do you need?

To figure out how much you will need, set up the ratio you know and next to it the ratio you want, with a question mark for the missing piece. $\frac{2}{3} = \frac{12}{?}$ We'll put the equal sign in there, even though there's still a number missing, to remind you that you want the two ratios to be equal.

You are looking for a bottom number that will make that second ratio equal to the first. The way to do this is to figure out what you multiplied the 2 by to get 12, and then to multiply the 3 on the bottom by that. You're actually multiplying the ratio by some number over itself, which always equals 1, so the ratio stays the same. See how the same things keep coming up? Since $2 \times 6 = 12$, multiply $\frac{2}{3} \times \frac{6}{6}$.

$$\frac{2}{3} \times \frac{6}{6} = \frac{12}{18}$$

The ratios 2 : 3 and 12 : 18 are equal ratios, so they form a proportion. That tells you that if you use 12 ounces of grape juice, you'll need 18 ounces of apple juice to make the punch correctly. You'll have $12 + 18 = 30$ ounces of punch all together.

The second method of solving a proportion is called cross-multiplying. Remember the trick we learned for comparing fractions to see which is bigger? You multiplied the numbers diagonally across from each other, and put the answers above the numerators. To compare $\frac{5}{6}$ and $\frac{12}{16}$, for example, you multiply 16×5 and put the answer of 80 over the 5, and then multiply 6×12 and put the answer over the 12. The fraction with the bigger number above it is the bigger fraction.

$$\overset{80}{\frac{5}{6}} \times \overset{72}{\frac{12}{16}}$$

What if you have a proportion, like $\frac{1}{2} = \frac{4}{8}$, where the fractions are equal?

$$\overset{8}{\frac{1}{2}} \times \overset{8}{\frac{4}{8}}$$

Since the fractions are equal, the little answers above them are equal. That's what we'll use to help solve the proportion.

Let's try solving the proportion $3 : 7 = ? : 56$. Set up the ratio you know and next to it the ratio you want, with a question mark for the missing piece. To find the missing piece, multiply in 2 diagonals.

$$\overset{56 \times 3}{\frac{3}{7}} = \overset{7 \times ?}{\frac{?}{56}}$$

This is called **cross-multiplying**. 56×3 is 168 so 7 times the missing piece has to be 168. To find out what the missing piece is, you divide 168 by 7, and $168 \div 7 = 24$. The missing piece is 24.

This exact same problem might also look like this. $3 : 7 :: ? : 56$. Those middle four dots are the proportion sign, and this is the same proportion as before. The outsides of the proportion, 3 and 56, are called the **extremes**. The insides are called the **means**. If you multiply the extremes by each other, their product will equal the product of the means. The product of the means is always equal to the product of the extremes.

$$\overbrace{3 : 7}^{\text{Extremes}} :: \underbrace{? : 56}_{\text{Means}}$$

When you set up proportions to find a missing piece, you can set them up in a variety of ways. If you are saying, for example, that you want a mud recipe that is 2 parts water to 3 parts dirt and you have 12 cups of dirt, you can set it up two ways. The first way we have already seen. The ratios are placed side by side. All you have to do is make sure both ratios are in the same order, in this case, dirt over water.

$$\frac{2 \text{ dirt}}{3 \text{ water}} = \frac{12 \text{ dirt}}{? \text{ water}}$$

The other way is to have the dirt all on one side, and all the water on the other side. Again, order matters. If we put dirt over available dirt, then we must put water over available water.

$$\frac{2 \text{ dirt}}{12 \text{ dirt}} = \frac{3 \text{ water}}{? \text{ water}}$$

Try to cross-multiply both ways. You always get $36 = 2 \times ?$ The missing piece is 18, because 36 divided by 2 is 18. Any way you slice it, you have the piece you are looking for. As long as you keep on top of the order, you can organize a lot of math any way you want.

A lot of problems about ratio and proportion have to do with how much of a mixture you want to make. Suppose that you know that for a particular lemonade recipe, the ratio is 12 parts syrup to 2 parts lemon juice, and say you wanted to make 28 gallons of lemonade. How much syrup and juice would you need? Well, you know the ratio is set up part to part. If the lemonade ratio is 12 to 2, the whole is $12 + 2 = 14$ parts.

The whole is 14. Now you can set up what is called a **ratio box**. A ratio box helps make ratios more explicit. You put in the ratio and the whole, and then the amount you want.

Ratio Box	Part (Syrup)	Part (Lemon Juice)	Whole
Basic ratio	12	2	14
Multiplied by			
Total			28

Now what was 14 multiplied by to become 28? (Here is yet another reason to memorize your times tables.) Fourteen was multiplied by 2 to become 28. Put 2 in the "multiplied by" slot.

Ratio Box	Part (Syrup)	Part (Lemon Juice)	Whole
Basic ratio	12	2	14
Multiplied by			2
Total			28

The cool thing is, whatever the whole was multiplied by, the parts were multiplied by that too, because the ratio will always stay the same, no matter how many millions of gallons of a mixture you want to make. Multiply the parts by 2 to see how many you will need.

Ratio Box	Part (Syrup)	Part (Lemon Juice)	Whole
Basic ratio	12	2	14
Multiplied by	2	2	2
Total	24	4	28

Twenty-four gallons of syrup and 4 gallons of lemon juice will make 28 gallons of this lemonade. Now here's the kicker. Add the 24 and the 4 together. They add up to the 28 gallons of lemonade! You can check yourself by making sure the parts add up to the whole.

You can use the ratio box even if you are looking for only part. Say you wanted to make lemonade and only had 6 cups of lemon juice.

Ratio Box	Part (Syrup)	Part (Lemon Juice)	Whole
Basic ratio	12	2	14
Multiplied by			
Total		6	

Since there were 6 cups of lemon juice, you know you multiplied the 2 by 3 to get the 6. You just multiply everything else by 3.

Ratio Box	Part (Syrup)	Part (Lemon Juice)	Whole
Basic ratio	12	2	14
Multiplied by	3	3	3
Total	36	6	42

QUIZ #8

PROPORTIONS AND RATIOS

1. Simplify the ratio 4 : 6.

2. Find the missing piece in the proportion 2 : 3::8 : ?

3. Find the missing piece in the proportion $\dfrac{4}{5} = \dfrac{12}{?}$.

4. Find the missing piece in the proportion $\dfrac{3}{4} = \dfrac{6}{?}$.

5. Find the missing piece in the proportion $\dfrac{10}{11} = \dfrac{3}{?}$.

6. If Sondra has a box with 4 cassettes and 8 compact discs in it, what is the ratio of compact discs to cassettes in the box? Put the ratio in its most reduced form.

7. Taylor is trying to make cement with only sand and water, and is using 3 cups of sand for every 2 cups of water. If he wants to make 15 cups of this (not very successful) cement, how much water will he need?

8. Taylor is making glue out of flour and water. (This actually works! You can try it yourself.) He uses 1 tablespoon of water for every 3 tablespoons of flour, and he makes 12 tablespoons of glue. How many tablespoons of flour did he use?

9. Taylor and Jennifer own a book collection. The books are fiction and nonfiction. The ratio of fiction to nonfiction is 2 : 1. If they own 21 books altogether, how many fiction books are in the collection?

10. Jennifer wants to create a delicious sundae. She has heard that you should mix ice cream and hot fudge in a ratio of 3 to 1. If she wants to make 16 gallons of the sundae, how much hot fudge will she need?

ooooooooooo

Jennifer was still giggling over the notion of a quarter-inch-high inch high model of Sondra. "Can you picture that, Taylor?" she asked. "Taylor?" Jennifer and Sondra turned in slow circles, looking for Taylor. "Taylor?" Jennifer called once more, just a little louder.

"Look at this," Taylor's muffled voice called from behind the enclosed city model. "This is cool."

Sondra and Jennifer followed the sound of Taylor's voice until they found him bent over a display case on the history of the city.

"Did you know that our city is really two cities?" Taylor asked. "The original city was incorporated in 1912," he read from the placard on top of the case, "and in 1956, the city charter was revised to include surrounding areas that had been built up over the years." Drawings and photos showed the original and the expanded city.

Sondra read from the information at the other end of the case. "The original city covered only 30 percent of the current 120 square miles."

Thirty percent? You might be wondering what a percent is. Well, percents are just fractions. Do you remember how decimals are a smaller group of fractions whose denominators are powers of 10? Well, percents are an even smaller group of fractions. Percents are fractions with denominators of 100. Remember when we talked about *cent* meaning *one hundred*? Well, *percent* means *per 100* and *per* means *for each* or *out of*, so 30 percent means 30 for every 100 parts. Thirty percent, also written as 30%, is actually $\frac{30}{100}$.

All percents can be translated into fractions with denominators of 100, so 30% is equal to $\frac{30}{100}$. You can also reduce the fraction to a smaller fraction. $\frac{30}{100} = \frac{3}{10}$.

How can you translate a percent into a decimal? Drop the percent sign and move the decimal point 2 spaces to the left.

$$60\% \text{ becomes } 0.60$$

$$2\% \text{ becomes } 0.02$$

Try converting 35%. Make it into a decimal first. Drop the percent sign and move the decimal point two spaces to the left.

$$35\% \Rightarrow 0.35 \Rightarrow \frac{35}{100}$$

Now, as a fraction, 35% is $\frac{35}{100}$. Can you reduce it?

$$\frac{35}{100} \div \frac{5}{5} = \frac{7}{20}.$$

You can also convert a fraction into a percent. Multiply the fraction by 1, in the form of a number over itself, to provide a denominator of 100.

Let's try to convert $\frac{2}{25}$ into a percent. What number could you multiply 25 by to get 100? To find the answer, divide 100 by 25, and you get 4. Multiply $\frac{2}{25}$ by $\frac{4}{4}$.

$$\frac{2}{25} \times \frac{4}{4} = \frac{8}{100}$$

This is 8 out of 100, or 8%. You can also look at it as a decimal of 0.08, because it is 8 hundredths.

To convert a decimal into a percent, just move the decimal point over 2 places to the right and add a percent sign. For instance, 0.08 becomes 008. or 8, add the percent sign and you are back to 8%.

By the way, when you have 100% of something, how much do you have? You have the whole thing. One hundred percent is equal to 1, or the whole.

CONVERSION

1. Convert $\dfrac{1}{2}$ to a decimal and a percent.

2. Convert $\dfrac{3}{4}$ to a decimal and a percent.

3. Convert 0.40 to a fraction and a percent.

4. Convert 30% to a decimal and a fraction.

5. Convert 20% to a decimal and a fraction.

6. Convert 29% to a decimal and a fraction.

7. Convert $\dfrac{7}{10}$ to a decimal and a percent.

8. Convert $\dfrac{3}{50}$ to a decimal and a percent.

9. Convert 0.23 to a fraction and a percent.

10. Convert 0.001 to a fraction and a percent.

ooooooooooooo

"Thirty percent of the current 120 square miles," Taylor repeated, squinting a little. "Just how big is that?"

"What do you mean?" Jennifer asked.

"Percents are fractions, right?" Taylor didn't wait for an answer. "So the original city was a fraction of 120 square miles, less than 120 square miles, but how big was it? How many square miles?"

OOOOOOOOOOOO

The key to the answer to Taylor's question is the word *of*. The word *of* means *times* in math language, so what Taylor wants to know is, what is 30% times 120? To answer this, convert the 30% to either a decimal or a fraction and then multiply. 30% × 120 becomes

$$\frac{30}{100} \times 120 = \frac{30}{{}_5\cancel{100}} \times \frac{\cancel{120}^6}{1} = \frac{\cancel{30}^6}{\cancel{5}_1} \times \frac{6}{1} = \frac{36}{1} \text{ or 36 square miles.}$$

OOOOOOOOOOOO

"Thirty six square miles," Taylor thought out loud. "That doesn't sound like very much." He turned to Sondra and Jennifer. "Do you know how big that is?"

"Well," Jennifer stalled, then admitted, "no." Taylor looked disappointed.

"Maybe we can use the model to get some idea," Sondra said. She led the way back around to the viewing platform and waved a hand toward the miniature city. "If we could find something in the city to compare to, something that we know the size of, we could get a feeling for how big the original city was."

The three of them stared at the model for a few minutes. "What about One Tree Park?" Jennifer asked. "We've certainly hung out there enough to have a sense of how big that is. Does anybody know how many square miles the park covers?"

"I think I saw that on one of the posters," Taylor said. The three kids moved from display to display until Taylor found the information they wanted. "One Tree Park is 1.8 square miles of rolling lawns, punctuated by the giant oak for which it is named."

"OK," Jennifer squinted. "One Tree Park is 1.8 square miles, and the original city was 36 square miles. So how do they compare?"

$$\bullet\bullet\bullet\bullet\bullet\bullet\bullet\bullet\bullet\bullet\bullet\bullet\bullet$$

The basic question the kids asked was, the park is what part of the original city? You can answer that question in several different ways. You can think about fractions: The park is what fraction of the original city? Or you can think in ratios: What is the ratio of the park's size to the original city's size? Or you can use percents: The park is what percent of the original city?

Fractions, ratios, and percents are all connected, of course. To find a percent, you often use a proportion, which is made from 2 equal ratios. Let's answer this question with a percent, and use a rule, given in the form of a proportion, that's useful for many percent questions.

$$\frac{\text{part}}{\text{whole}} = \frac{\%}{100}$$

Our question is: the park is what part of the original city? The park, which covers 1.8 square miles, is the part, and the original city, 36 square miles, is the whole. The % is what we're trying to find, and the fourth number is always 100. Set up the proportion and cross multiply.

$$\frac{1.8}{36} = \frac{?}{100}$$
$$36 \times ? = 1.8 \times 100$$
$$36 \times ? = 180$$
$$? = 180 \div 36 = 5$$

The park is 5% of the size of the original city.

Many percent problems can be set up using this same rule. In this problem, we had to find the percent, when we knew the part and the whole. If you are asked to find 25% of 280, you know the percent and the whole, and you need to find the part, so your proportion is $\frac{\text{part}}{280} = \frac{25}{100}$. You still cross-multiply to solve the proportion. Another question might ask: 12 is 60% of what number? You know the part and the percent, and you need to find the whole, so the proportion is $\frac{12}{\text{whole}} = \frac{60}{100}$.

If you have trouble deciding which number goes where, you might want to remember the rule as $\frac{\text{is}}{\text{of}} = \frac{\%}{100}$ instead of $\frac{\text{part}}{\text{whole}} = \frac{\%}{100}$. The word *is* will always appear near the part, and the word *of* will be near the whole. Of course, the % sign will usually be on the percent.

$$\overbrace{15 \text{ is}}^{\text{Part}} \quad \overbrace{\text{what percent}}^{\%} \quad \overbrace{\text{of } 6\,0?}^{\text{Whole}}$$

$$\overbrace{20 \text{ is}}^{\text{Part}} \quad \overbrace{45\%}^{\%} \quad \overbrace{\text{of what number}?}^{\text{Whole}}$$

$$\overbrace{\text{What is}}^{\text{Part}} \quad \overbrace{90\%}^{\%} \quad \overbrace{\text{of } 14\,6?}^{\text{Whole}}$$

THINK ABOUT THIS

The rules for multiples of 10% are cool and easy. One hundred percent of something is the whole thing. To find 10%, you just move the decimal point one space over to the left. For 1%, you move the decimal point 2 spaces to the left. How about for 0.1%? What do you think? You move the decimal point three spaces over to the left. Pretty cool, huh?

$$100\% \text{ of } 2{,}356 = 2{,}356$$

$$10\% \text{ of } 2{,}356 = 235.6$$

$$1\% \text{ of } 2{,}356 = 23.56$$

$$0.1\% \text{ of } 2{,}356 = 2.356$$

And so on.

OOOOOOOOOOOO

"From 36 square miles to 120 square miles in a little over 40 years," Taylor thought out loud. "That's a big change."

Jennifer concentrated on subtracting 36 from 120. "84 square miles," she said.

"So the amount the city grew," Sondra said, "is more than twice its original size."

"You mean the city grew more than 100%?" Jennifer asked.

"More than 200%," Taylor corrected.

OOOOOOOOOOOO

To determine the percent change, first find the change. In this case, there is an 84 square mile gain. Next compare the change to the original number by setting up a proportion.

$$\frac{\text{change}}{\text{original}} = \frac{\%}{100}$$

$$\frac{84}{36} = \frac{?}{100}$$

You can cross-multiply again.

$$8400 = 36 \times \,?$$

$$8400 \div 36 = 233\tfrac{1}{3}$$

The city had a percent increase in size of $233\tfrac{1}{3}\%$.

YOU CAN ALSO THINK ABOUT THIS

Say you are looking at a multiple of 10%. Someone wants to know what 30% of 200 is. One quick way to do it is to find 10% of 200. Just move that decimal point over 1 place to the left; 10% of 200 is 20. Then, since you want 30% and not 10%, just multiply that 10% by 3.

$$20 \times 3 = 60$$

Since 10% times 3 is 30%, 60 is 30% of 200. There are often different ways to do a math problem; the more ways you can think of, the more comfortable with math you will be.

QUIZ #10

PERCENTAGES

1. 10% of 50 =

2. 25% of 16 =

3. 3% of 300 =

4. $\dfrac{23}{50} = \dfrac{?}{100}$

5. $\dfrac{2}{25} = \dfrac{?}{100}$

6. If Sondra has 10 carrots and she gives 90% of them to her sister, how many carrots does she have left?

7. Taylor receives 32% of $1,200 as a prize in a raffle. How much money does he win?

8. Taylor offers 100% of nothing to his little brother as payment for mowing the lawn. Is it a good deal for Taylor's little brother, and how much will he get?

9. Taylor and Jennifer have 3 out of 30 possible baseball cards. What percent of the baseball cards do they have?

10. The owner of a famous collection of 200 bats loses 1 bat to Jennifer. Her bat represents what percentage loss to the collection?

○○○○○○○○○○○○

Taylor, Jennifer, and Sondra started to make their way toward the exit of the exhibit hall, chatting about what to see next and remarking on how wonderful the air-conditioning felt.

"Whoa!" Taylor called to the girls, sliding behind them to study a small case against the wall. Jennifer and Sondra joined him there.

"Do you think that's real?" Jennifer asked after she had read a little of the display.

"I've never heard of tunnels under the city," Sondra said with a shake of her head.

Taylor continued reading. "It says a lot of people think it's just a legend, but the story goes back as far as there have been records. A network of tunnels under the city, and a challenge that anyone who can travel all the tunnels without visiting any tunnel a second time will receive special honors."

"But if there really were tunnels," Sondra asked, "don't you think someone would have seen them?"

Jennifer looked startled. She swallowed hard before she spoke. "I think we did, this afternoon."

REVIEW

1. Rewrite 20% as a fraction and a decimal.

2. $\dfrac{2}{3} = \dfrac{8}{?}$

3. $1 : 3 :: 2 : ?$

4. Rewrite $\dfrac{1}{4}$ as a decimal and a percent.

5. Rewrite $\dfrac{3}{20}$ as a decimal and a percent.

6. Jennifer needs to buy ink for a special invisible-writing mixture. If the mixture has water to ink in a ratio of 2 to 3, how many cups of ink are there in 25 cups of the mixture? What percentage of the mixture is ink?

7. Taylor has to give 14% of his collection of 200 marbles to his little brother (parental punishment after the lawn mower incident). How many marbles does he have to give away?

8. If Jennifer makes pretzels using 3 drops of red food coloring for every 1 drop of yellow food coloring (to make them look brown when they dry), how many pints of red food coloring will she need to make 16 pints of brown coloring? What percentage of the mixture is yellow food coloring?

9. Jennifer makes 10 gallons of salt water, which is 50% salt, and 50% water. What is the ratio of salt to water in the mixture?

10. Jennifer bought a set of trucks and cars in a ratio of 1 to 5. If there are 15 cars, how many trucks are there in the set?

CHAPTER 6

Probability and Averages

"What do you mean, we've seen the tunnels?" Sondra asked. She waved her hand in front of Jennifer, who was staring into space. "What tunnels have we seen?"

Jennifer shook her head to clear it. "Not the tunnels, exactly," she explained, "but maybe the entrance to the tunnels." She turned to Taylor. "Do you remember that door we saw in the storeroom? The one Mr. Ippolitto said that no one ever uses?"

Taylor wrinkled his nose in disbelief. "Come on! It's just a door. Don't you think that's an awfully big leap?"

"Maybe," Jennifer conceded, "but think about it. The storeroom is below ground. The shop is in the center of the old city. Why else would that door be there?"

"Why would a door be there?" Sondra turned the question around. "Yes, it is in the original city, but so are lots of other buildings. Why would the door be there? And is it the door? Are there other doors? Does it matter which one you use? How big are these tunnels? And how are they laid out? And…"

"OK, OK!" Jennifer cut her off. "Forget I said anything!"

"I'm not saying 'no,'" Sondra explained. "I think the idea is interesting. I just think we've got a lot of research to do before we know what we're doing, or if there really is anything to do."

"So how do we do this research?" Taylor asked.

Sondra thought for a moment. "Let's see if we can get into the museum's library."

Mrs. Bridge, the silver-haired librarian, seemed only a little surprised by the three young visitors. The museum library looked like little more than a wood paneled room, furnished with a few tables topped by reading lamps and the desk at which Mrs. Bridge greeted them.

"I wondered if that new exhibit would stir up interest in the old stories," she said after the kids explained why they had come.

"Do you think they're just stories?" Taylor asked.

Mrs. Bridge smiled in Taylor's direction, but the look in her eyes seemed far away. "Just stories?" she said after a minute. "Oh, I couldn't say, but certainly over the years, there have been plenty of people who have taken them seriously."

"Really?" Jennifer's face lit up.

"We'd be interested in knowing who, if you know," Sondra said, "or at least how many people thought the stories were real."

"I'll see what information we have," Mrs. Bridge agreed. "What other questions are you trying to answer?" she asked. "If I know that, it will help me choose materials from the archives for you."

Sondra, Jennifer, and Taylor blurted out all their questions about the stories of the city tunnels, and Mrs. Bridge made notes on a slip of paper. When they finally ran out of ideas, the librarian invited them to make themselves comfortable at one of the tables, and then disappeared through a door in the back wall. The kids seated themselves around the nearest table, leaving the seat closest to the librarian's desk empty. In a few moments, Mrs. Bridge reappeared, her arms full of books and portfolios, and set the materials on the table.

"This should get you started. These are maps of the city and building records," she explained, laying her hands on some of the folders. "And these histories all make reference to the tunnel stories."

The three kids thanked her and set right to work examining the materials. Jennifer grabbed the maps, Sondra dove into the history books, and Taylor started combing through the building records.

"If I'm reading this correctly," Taylor said after a few minutes, "there are 300 buildings from the original city still standing."

"So that means, assuming there's one entrance to the tunnels, that there's a 1 in 300 probability that we've found the door," Jennifer said, looking up from her maps.

"Well," Sondra ran her finger over the page in front of her as she spoke, "we can't be sure how reliable this book is, but according to this there are 4 entrances, in different parts of the city. So that means the probability of finding a door is $\dfrac{4}{300}$ or $\dfrac{1}{75}$."

○○○○○○○○○○○○

Probability is the mathematical way people talk about the likelihood that something will happen. It is usually expressed in fraction form and is used to figure the chances of random events occurring. **Random events** are events with outcomes we have no real control over, such as flipping a coin.

One chance in 300 would look like this: $\frac{1}{300}$. The top part indicates how many successful possibilities there are, and the bottom part indicates the number of total possibilities. This particular probability is small, so it tells us that there is a small chance of finding the door. It also implies that the opposite—not finding the door—is very likely to happen. They would have a $\frac{299}{300}$ chance of not finding the door.

The bigger the fraction, the more likely a successful outcome is. The smaller the fraction, the less likely the successful outcome is. If the report of 4 doors is true, there are 4 successes, 4 doors to the tunnels out of 300 buildings. As a fraction, that's $\frac{4}{300}$, which reduces to $\frac{1}{75}$. Since $\frac{1}{75}$ is a larger number than $\frac{1}{300}$, the kids have a better chance of finding the door if there are 4 entrances.

The maximum probability is 1. A sure thing has a probability of 1. Out of a million chances, it will happen every time. Say you flipped a 2-headed coin 1 million times. The coin will land on heads every time, so the probability of getting heads is $\frac{1,000,000}{1,000,000}$. Something that has already happened has a probability of 1, but people don't often talk about the probability of things that have already happened. Probability is the branch of mathematics that deals with uncertainty. What already happened is certain.

It's also possible to be sure that something *won't* happen. The probability of getting tails when you are flipping a two-headed coin is 0. Out of 1 million flips, none are tails, so the probability of tails is $\frac{0}{1,000,000}$. The minimum probability is zero, so probabilities are always numbers between 0 and 1.

⊙⊙⊙⊙⊙⊙⊙⊙⊙⊙⊙⊙

"Now, wait a minute," Jennifer said, "let's think about this. There are 300 buildings and 4 doors to the tunnels."

"Maybe," Sondra cautioned.

"Yeah, yeah, I know, but let's just say it's so. Does every building have a door? Are we looking at 4 good doors out of 300 doors, or are we saying that 4 of the 300 buildings have doors? If only 4 of the buildings have doors, then the fact that we know Mr. Ippolitto's storeroom has a door is a very good sign."

Taylor frowned. "Why don't we just go open the door and look? If it's a door to the tunnels, we're in. If it's not..." His voice trailed off.

"If it's not, there are 299 other buildings to look at," Jennifer said. "But our chances are 4 in 299, instead of 4 in 300. That's at least a little better."

⊙⊙⊙⊙⊙⊙⊙⊙⊙⊙⊙⊙

The truth is that Jennifer is right. If they checked and found out that the door at Mr. Ippolitto's was not a door to the tunnels, there would still be

4 successful doors, but only 299 possible locations for them. The chance that the next building they looked at would have a door to the tunnels would be $\frac{4}{299}$. If they found out that Mr. Ippolitto's door *did* lead to the tunnels, they would know that there were three other doors somewhere in the remaining 299 buildings. In that case, the probability that the next building would also have a door to the tunnel would be $\frac{3}{299}$.

Checking to see if any one of the buildings had a door to the tunnels changes the probability for the next building you try. When one event, like opening the door, changes the probability of the next event, we say they are **dependent events**. The probability of the second event depends on the first one. If you have a bag that holds 3 red marbles and 4 blue marbles, and you pull out 1 marble without looking, the probability that the marble is blue is 4 out of 7 or $\frac{4}{7}$. What if you put that first marble in your pocket, and then pull another marble out of the bag. There are only 6 marbles in the bag now, not 7. How many are blue? Well, that depends. What color is the marble in your pocket? If it's blue, there are only 3 blue marbles left, so the chance that the second marble will be blue is $\frac{3}{6}$, but if the marble in your pocket is red, there are still 4 blue ones in the bag, and the probability that marble #2 will be blue is $\frac{4}{6}$. Because you kept that first marble in your pocket, the color of that marble has an effect on the probabilities for your second marble. When you draw more than 1 marble without replacement, the draws are dependent events.

If you had pulled out that first marble, noted its color, and then put it back in the bag before you pulled out the second one, the probabilities for the second draw would have been exactly the same as for the first draw. By putting the first marble back, you set all the conditions back the way they were at the beginning: same number of marbles, same number of reds, same number of blues. When you draw more than one marble with replacement, the draws are independent events.

Imagine tossing a fair coin, one that is equally likely to land heads or tails. Two separate flips are **independent events**. That means the first flip and the second flip have nothing to do with each other; they don't affect each other's outcome at all. After all, a coin has no memory of past events. It will flip randomly no matter what. Since there are 2 possible outcomes, and an equal chance of getting either, the probability of getting heads is $\frac{1}{2}$. No matter how many flips you do, each coin toss has the same probability of going heads or tails, provided you have a fair coin.

Often people think that getting a string of heads makes it more likely that they will get tails on the next toss. They feel that things ought to even out, and, in fact, things will even out or get close to the same number of heads and tails, but only after many, many, (many, many, many) tosses. If you've tossed a coin 10 times and the last 8 were heads, the probability that the next toss will land heads is exactly the same as it was on the first toss: $\frac{1}{2}$. Each toss is an independent event.

There are several ways to find the probability of several unrelated events. Let's say you were going to flip a coin three times and you wanted to know the probability that you would get all heads. One way to find out is to list them. How many possible outcomes are there?

HHH, HHT, HTH, HTT, TTT, TTH, THT, THH

There are 8 possible outcomes. What is the probability that you will get all heads? There is only 1 way out of 8 possible ways that this can happen, so the probability is $\frac{1}{8}$.

The way to do this quickly is to multiply the probabilities. That means the probability of getting heads on the first toss is $\frac{1}{2}$. The probability of getting heads on the second toss is $\frac{1}{2}$, and the same goes for the third toss. So the 3 probabilities are $\frac{1}{2}$, $\frac{1}{2}$, and $\frac{1}{2}$. To find the probabilities of getting all three heads, just multiply these.

$$\frac{1}{2} \times \frac{1}{2} \times \frac{1}{2} = \frac{1}{8}$$

This works for any set of independent events. If you have 2 separate bags, each with 1 red marble and 1 blue marble, and you choose 1 marble from each bag, what is the probability that both chosen marbles will be blue? Well, the probability that the marble chosen will be blue is $\frac{1}{2}$ in both cases, so the probability that both will be blue is $\frac{1}{2} \times \frac{1}{2}$, or $\frac{1}{4}$.

PROBABILITY

1. If you have a bag with 5 jellybeans in it—2 red, 2 orange, and 1 green—what is the probability that if you just stick your hand in and choose randomly, the jellybean you choose will be green?

2. In that same bag with the same 5 jellybeans in it, what is the probability that you will choose a red jellybean?

3. Using that same old bag of 5 jellybeans, find the probability that you will choose a white jellybean.

4. You now have 2 of those bags of jellybeans, and you are choosing 1 from the first bag and 1 from the second bag. What is the probability that both jellybeans will be green?

5. Using the same situation as in question 4, what is the probability that both jellybeans will be orange?

6. Poof! One bag of jellybeans just disappeared. Now you have just the 1 bag again, with 5 jellybeans in it—2 red, 2 orange and 1 green. You pick one jellybean, note its color, then put it back, shake up the bag, and choose another. What is the probability that both jellybeans are red?

7. If you draw 2 jellybeans as described in question 6, what is the probability that both are green?

8. You still have just that 1 bag. You pick 1 jellybean, note its color, and then choose another without putting the first 1 back. What is the probability that both jellybeans are orange?

9. Is that bag wearing out yet? You have that same 1 bag of jellybeans, and just like in question 7, you pick 1 jellybean and note its color, but you do not put it back in the bag before you pick a second one. What is the probability that you chose 1 green, then 1 red?

10. In the same situation described in questions 8 and 9, what is the probability that both jellybeans are green?

OOOOOOOOOOOOO

"But it's not just about finding a door," Sondra pointed out. "I mean, if you seriously want to take the challenge in the legend, you have to walk through all tunnels without repeating any section. That's going to take planning. It might not be possible at all, depending on how the tunnels are laid out, but if it is possible, it will probably be important to start in the right place."

"Huh?" It was the only word Taylor could find. "Why does it matter where we start?" he asked finally. "We just need to go all the way through, right?"

"Yes, but we don't know how the tunnel's laid out," Jennifer said. She looked down at the documents spread over the table in front of her. "So far, these maps are no help. We could really use at least a rough idea of the layout to try to plan a route."

"Why?" Taylor asked again, and the word sounded a lot like a whine.

Sondra flipped her paper over and drew a picture that looked like a house with an X through it. "Do you remember this puzzle?" she asked Taylor. "You have to trace it without lifting your pencil or going back over a line."

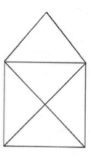

"Sure," Taylor said. "Everybody's done that. It's easy."

"It's easy, if you start in the right place," Sondra explained. "What if I said you had to start at the point of the roof?" Taylor made several attempts at tracing the picture before declaring that it couldn't be done. "The tunnel challenge may be just like that," Sondra explained. "If we start in the right place, we can do it, but if not, it's impossible."

"Except that the tunnels may be much more complicated," Jennifer added.

Taylor sighed and shook his head. "I don't know if it's possible to walk through the tunnels or not," he said, "but I'm starting to feel like it's impossible to keep track of everything we need to find out." He scrubbed his forehead with his arm. "Could we make a list, a plan, something?"

The girls agreed that would be a good idea, and Sondra borrowed a pencil and a sheet of paper from Mrs. Bridge. "OK," she said as she sat down again, "what are the things we need to do?"

"Well," Jennifer said, "we need to find a map of the tunnels, if there is one, so that we can plan a route." Sondra wrote MAP at the top of the paper.

"I can't believe someone built these tunnels just to drive people like us crazy," Taylor said. "It might help us to know what their actual purpose was." Sondra nodded and wrote PURPOSE.

"If we're going to try this," Sondra said, "we really need some idea of how long it will take and whether we need to take any supplies with us. I'd think water and flashlights, at least." She added SUPPLIES to the list.

"Has anyone tried this before?" Jennifer asked. "Are there any records or reports of what they did or how far they got? We might be able to learn from them."

"So, I'll add RECORDS to the list," Sondra said, "and I think we should try to find out how we prove that we've done it. How does anyone know if we're telling the truth?" She wrote VERIFY as she spoke, then waited quietly for the next idea. After a time, she realized no one was saying anything. "What else?" she asked.

Jennifer and Taylor exchanged glances, then looked back at Sondra with a shrug. "That's it?" Sondra asked, and the others nodded. "OK, we've got five tasks on the list. Now we've got to decide on the order we're going to tackle them."

When you are arranging things, putting things in order, or choosing things in such a way that the position matters, you're dealing with **permutations.** For example, if you're choosing an editor and an assistant editor for a club, order matters, but if you're choosing 2 co-editors to share a job, order won't matter. When you are choosing possible arrangements from a group or figuring out how many possible arrangements there are, those arrangements are called permutations.

If you are arranging just 2 or 3 things, one way to figure out the permutations is simply to work your way through them slowly, listing all the possibilities. Suppose you want to choose an editor and assistant editor from 5 candidates: Annie, Brad, Chris, Danielle, and Edward. We'll call them A, B, C, D, and E.

If you choose A first, that is, you choose Annie for editor, you can choose any of the other 4 as assistant editor. Your possibilities are AB, AC, AD, and AE, or four possibilities.

Now try to list all the possible combinations to combine with B: BA, BC, BD, BE. Four again. Remember: BA isn't the same as AB. We said that order mattered.

Now how many combinations can you make with the next letter, C? CA, CB, CD, CE. And D? DA, DB, DC, DE. Then all that is left is E and, as you can probably predict by now, there are 4 possibilities with E as well. EA, EB, EC, ED. Now add all the possibilities together. 4 + 4 + 4 + 4 + 4 = 20. There are 20 different possibilities (or permutations).

There is another way to determine the number of permutations, but if you ever get confused, you can always just list them like we did above. To figure them quickly, ask yourself how many possibilities there are for the first spot. In this case, how many people could be the editor? There are 5 people who could be chosen. Once you have written that down, count the possibilities for the second spot. Since the same person can't be both editor and assistant editor, there are only 4 possibilities. Multiply your 2 possibilities, and that's it. $5 \times 4 = 20$. That's how many permutations there are.

The kids have 5 choices for what to do first: MAP, PURPOSE, SUPPLIES, RECORDS, and VERIFY. We'll call them M, P, S, R, and V. They have to do them all, but they want to put them in some sort of order. How many different ways can they put these tasks in order?

Now you aren't choosing just 2 out of 5. You are trying to find the number of possible arrangements for all 5, but you do it the same way. How many possibilities are there for each space? There are 5 possibilities for what to do first, 4 choices for what to do second, 3 choices for the third spot, 2 for the next to last, and 1 for the last place. Now multiply $5 \times 4 \times 3 \times 2 \times 1 = 120$. There are 120 possible arrangements of the 5 activities.

In some situations, you have to choose, but the order in which you choose doesn't matter. Think about choosing co-editors. If you choose Annie and Brad or you choose Brad and Annie, the outcome is the same. How many different combinations are there?

Combinations. Pretty logical name, wouldn't you say? Well, again, let's call Annie, Brad, Chris, Danielle, and Edward by their initials to make things easier. As we did in the earlier example, start with the first choice, A. Now how many combinations can you have that start with A? AB, AC, AD, and AE. There are 4 possible combinations that begin with A.

How many possible combinations begin with B? Think about it carefully. BA? No, because if order doesn't matter, AB and BA are the same, and we already counted AB. The other possibilities are BC, BD, and BE, and those are OK. If we make an organized list and cross off the ones that are duplicates, it will be easier to count.

AB	AC	AD	AE
~~BA~~	BC	BD	BE
~~CA~~	~~CB~~	CD	CE
~~DA~~	~~DB~~	~~DC~~	DE
~~EA~~	~~EB~~	~~EC~~	~~ED~~

In this case, the number of combinations is half the number of permutations. The number of combinations will always be less than the number of permutations in a situation, but how much less will depend on the situation. Just as there's a quick way to find the number of permutations, there's an easy method to find the number of combinations. Imagine a fraction whose numerator is the number of permutations, and whose denominator has the same number of spaces to put numbers.

$$\frac{5 \times 4}{\_ \times \_}$$

Fill those spaces in the denominator with numbers in sequence starting from 1.

$$\frac{5 \times 4}{1 \times 2} = \frac{20}{2} = 10$$

The number of combinations of 7 things taken 3 at a time is

$$\frac{7 \times 6 \times 5}{1 \times 2 \times 3} = \frac{7 \times 6 \times 5}{6} = 35.$$

The strategy we use for counting permutations and combinations can be used in many situations. If your lunch counter offers 4 different sandwiches, 5 side dishes, and 3 drinks, and you choose one of each, there are $4 \times 5 \times 3$ or 60 different lunches you could choose.

QUIZ #13

PERMUTATIONS AND COMBINATIONS

1. Taylor has 3 flowers—a rose, a violet, and a peony. If he lines them up in a row on the counter, how many arrangements can he make?

2. Sondra is arranging prizes she won at the fair on the wall of her bedroom. She won 4 prizes, but she is putting only 2 on the wall of her room because she is saving the other 2 for the kitchen. How many possible arrangements of 2 prizes on her wall are there?

3. Taylor is building a spaceship. If there are 3 possible engines, 2 possible hull designs, and 2 possible interior designs, and he has to choose 1 of each to make a total spaceship plan. How many possible total spaceship plans are there?

4. Jennifer and Taylor are packing their ration box for a camping trip. There are 2 kinds of fruit, 3 kinds of bread, and 2 kinds of cheese to choose from, and they must only choose 1 of each. How many possible menus are there for the ration box?

5. Sondra is performing in a gymnastics competition, and she has to choose 3 moves from a group of 10 possible moves to arrange her opening sequence. None of the moves can be repeated. How many opening sequences are possible if she is choosing only from this group?

○○○○○○○○○○○○

"Even if we can find a map of these tunnels," Jennifer said, paging through the documents before her. "How will we know how long it's going to take us to get through them?"

Taylor was thinking. "Well, if we can figure out the distance we'll have to walk from start to finish and divide it by our walking speed, that should give us the time—or at least an idea of the time."

Sondra wedged the task list into the book she was reading before she looked up. "That sounds right," she said, "assuming we know how fast we walk." She thought for a minute. "We all live about a mile from school. How long does it take us to walk to school?"

"I'd say, maybe 20 minutes," Taylor said.

"You're pokey," Jennifer said. "I can do it 15 minutes, easily. Twelve if I'm late for homeroom."

"I'm somewhere in between, I guess," Sondra said. "I'd say it takes me about 17 or 18 minutes. So what's our average time?"

"16.4 minutes," Jennifer said.

"17 minutes," said Taylor.

"Beg your pardon?" Sondra asked.

OOOOOOOOOOOO

An **average** is a number expressing the middle of a group of numbers. There are several kinds of averages, but the one most people think of when they hear that word is also called the **arithmetic mean**. To find the mean of a group of numbers, add all the numbers in the group and then divide by how many numbers are in the group.

Jennifer added all the times they had mentioned, then divided by how many numbers are in the group, in this case, 5. Jennifer found an average time of $\dfrac{12+15+17+18+20}{5} = \dfrac{82}{5} = 16.4$ minutes.

What if Jennifer had taken only the slowest time for each of them? What is their average time now? You find an average by adding the numbers in the group and then dividing by how many numbers are in the group, so 15 + 18 + 20 = 53. Now you divide by how many numbers are in the group. There are 3 this time. Their average time is $53 \div 3 = 17\dfrac{2}{3}$ minutes.

So how did Taylor get an average time of 17 minutes? Was he just wrong? Well, making a mistake is always a possibility, it's more likely that Taylor calculated the median instead of the mean.

What is a **median**? In a set of numbers ordered from smallest to largest, the median is the middle number. Arranged in order, the times the kids gave were 12, 15, 17, 18, and 20. The median time is 17 minutes, because 17 is the number in the middle.

What if there is an even number of samples in the group? For instance, suppose we ignore Jennifer's claim that she can do it in 12 minutes, since she'd probably be running, not walking, if she were late for homeroom. Now you have 4 numbers to think about: 15, 17, 18, and 20. Find the two middle numbers—17 and 18—and then find their mean, 17.5.

THINK ABOUT THIS

What do you think is the fastest time in which the 100-yard dash has even been run? Would you believe 9.79 seconds? That's 300 feet in 9.79 seconds, which—if a runner could actually maintain that speed—would be equivalent to running a mile in 2.82 minutes.

There is a third kind of average, called the **mode**. What is a mode? The mode is the number that appears *most frequently* in a group of numbers. Since no number appears more than once in the times that Jennifer, Taylor and Sondra gave, their set of times has no mode.

What is the mode of this set of numbers?

7, 3, 6, 5, 6, 19

The mode of that set of numbers is 6, because 6 appears twice, while all the other numbers appear only once.

How about this next set of numbers?

4, 8, 9, 8, 4, 5, 7, 4, 9

The mode of that set is 4, because it appears 3 times, as opposed to 8 and 9, which appear only twice each.

AVERAGE, MEDIAN, AND MODE

1. What is the mean of 2, 3, and 4?

2. What is the mean of 3 and 7?

3. What is the mean of 1, 3, 6, 3, and 7?

4. What is the median of the group of numbers in question 3?

5. What is the mode of the group of numbers in question 3?

6. On Monday, Sondra biked 3 miles. On Tuesday, she biked 6 miles, and on Wednesday, she biked 15 miles. What was the average number of miles that Sondra biked per day over those 3 days?

7. Sondra, who was on some kind of physical fitness kick, did 14 push-ups on Thursday, 12 push-ups on Friday and 10 push-ups on Saturday. How many pushups did Sondra average per day over Thursday, Friday, and Saturday? Also, just to approximate, would her average increase or decrease if you just took the average of Thursday and Saturday?

8. Taylor is checking out prices on hats, because the sun has been bothering him recently. At the hat store, he looks at 6 hats. One of them is 2 dollars, 2 of them are 3 dollars each, 2 of them are 4 dollars each, and 1 of them is 8 dollars. What is the average price of the hats Taylor looks at?

9. Taylor and Jennifer are counting how many people on average live in the 7 houses on their block. 3 of the houses hold 8 people each, and the other 4 houses hold 1 person each. How many people live in the average house on their block?

10. Jennifer is measuring how high she can jump. She jumps 5 times, and these are the heights of her jumps: 20 inches, 29 inches, 26 inches, 20 inches, and 25 inches. What is the average height of her jumps? What is the mode? What is the median?

⦿⦿⦿⦿⦿⦿⦿⦿⦿⦿⦿⦿

By the way, can you tell how fast Jennifer, Taylor and Sondra walk? Just think back to proportions for a minute. If Jennifer went 1 mile, or 5,280 feet, in 12 minutes, how fast was she going per minute? Well, set up a proportion.

$$\frac{5280}{12} = \frac{?}{1}$$

Cross-multiply.

$$12 \times ? = 5280 \times 1.$$

Now divide.

$$\frac{5280}{12} = 440 \text{ feet per minute.}$$

Most rates are just proportions. Since rates are usually given as miles per hour or yards per second, you can remember back to percents, where you learned that "per" means divide. Just divide whenever it says "per," and that is your rate. But be careful not to forget about terms of measurement. If you are changing units of measurement, say seconds to minutes or minutes to hours, just set up the equation as a proportion instead of dividing. A proportion will always work if you set it up correctly.

AVERAGE

1. In a bag with 20 marbles, 10 red and 10 black, what is the probability that Rose will choose a green marble?

2. If Rose must choose 1 marble at random from a bag with 20 marbles in it (5 red, 3 blue, 10 green, and 2 yellow), what is the probability that the marble she chooses will be blue?

3. Rose is choosing marbles at random from that bag with 20 marbles in it (5 red, 3 blue, 10 green, and 2 yellow). If she draws 3 marbles, and she does not replace marbles after she draws them, what is the probability that she will draw 3 green marbles?

4. If Lionel has a box with 10 balls in it, 5 blue and 5 red, and he chooses a ball at random, what is the probability that the ball he chooses will be red?

5. If Sondra chooses a ball from a box that contains 10 blue balls, what is the probability that the ball she chooses will be blue?

6. Two years ago Sondra was 50 inches tall, last year Sondra was 53 inches tall, and this year Sondra is 56 inches tall. What is Sondra's mean height over the past 3 years?

7. Taylor has three snorkeling masks. One of the masks weighs 16 ounces, the second weighs 18 ounces, and the third weighs 20 ounces. What is the mean weight of the 3 masks?

8. Taylor is making a tape for a friend and is trying to decide which 3 songs to put first, and in what order, out of 7 songs. How many possible arrangements are there for the first 3 songs?

9. Jennifer swam 1 mile 5 times last week, when she was visiting her cousin at the ocean. Her times for each mile were: 20 minutes, 23 minutes, 20 minutes, 24 minutes, and 18 minutes. What was her mean time per mile, and the mode, and the median of her times?

10. Jennifer has a box with 1 blue marble, 1 green marble, and 1 red marble in it. (There sure are a lot of strange boxes of marbles around, don't you think?) If she chooses a marble at random and then replaces it 4 times in a row, what is the probability that she will choose a blue marble all 4 times?

CHAPTER 7

Charts and Graphs

Sondra had placed half a dozen more bookmarks in the history books by the time Mrs. Bridge came back over to their table. She whispered, although she and Sondra, Taylor, and Jennifer were the only ones in the library.

"When you 3 are ready to take a break from what you're reading, I've found some things on the computer that you might want to see."

Jennifer quickly folded the map she'd been examining. "Computer?"

Taylor closed his book and echoed the word. Mrs. Bridge led them to a computer workstation on the far side of her desk. "We don't save newspapers and magazine anymore," she explained quietly as they crossed the room. "All the content is saved in electronic files on the computer. I've done a few searches related to your questions, and found some articles you may find interesting."

Taylor slid into the chair in front of the computer and enlarged the first window, revealing an article from the local paper dated January 2000. It recounted the legend of the tunnels and included reports of attempts to navigate the tunnels, although none of the stories could be verified. What attracted the attention of all 3 kids was the graph that accompanied the article.

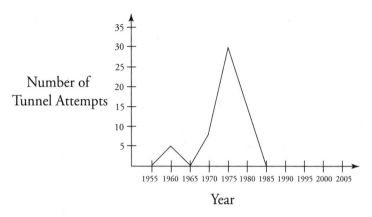

Year

"Look at that spike in 1975!" Jennifer exclaimed. She clamped a hand over her mouth when she realized how loud she had been. "What caused that?" she wondered, more quietly.

"Possibly the museum exhibit in 1974," Mrs. Bridge suggested. "It wasn't as extensive as the current installation, but it did mention the tunnel legend."

"But there was nothing after 1985," Taylor pointed out, "at least as far as the graph goes."

○○○○○○○○○○○○

A **line graph** uses lines to show information. The horizontal line, which goes left and right, is where the year is shown on this graph. It is sometimes called the **x-axis.** The vertical line, which goes up and down, is where the number of attempts is recorded on this graph. It is sometimes called the **y-axis.** To read a line graph, start at one of the **axes** (that's plural for *axis* and pronounced acks-eez). Say you wanted to know how many attempts to navigate the tunnels were made in 1970. Look at the 1970 spot on the horizontal axis and follow it up till you see the graphed line. Then look to the left to see how many attempts correspond with the place graphed. There were approximately 10 attempts in 1970.

Often the axes will show not the actual numbers, but a **scale** of the actual numbers. For example, a graph might show the hours of the day, and the *hundreds* of visitors to the museum. The graph below shows that at 3 P.M., the museum admitted not 4 visitors, but *400* people.

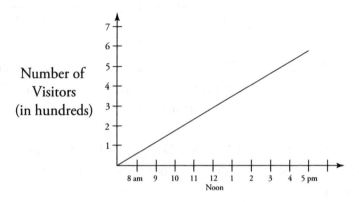

To make your own line graph, draw two lines on a piece of paper. Then label the axes. Make a height graph for yourself, from age 5 to age 12 (or whatever age you are now). Make the horizontal line "age" and the vertical line "height" because height depends on age. The information represented on the vertical axis usually depends on the information on the horizontal axis. Now, starting with 5, put your age, in years, at equal distances apart on that line. Then put inches on the other axis, starting below your height at age 5, to make it look good.

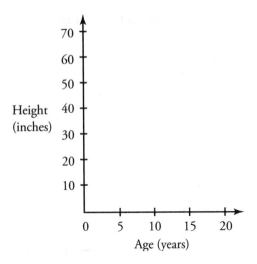

Now you can plot points. That means to put a mark on the graph for your height at each age. The person whose heights we are graphing was 30 inches tall at age 5, 32 inches at 6, 36 inches at 7, 38 inches at 8, 40 inches at 9, 42 inches at 10, 45 inches at 11, and 50 inches at 12.

To plot your own points, first go to the age. Then look to the left axis for the corresponding height. Mark the intersection of height and age with a dark point.

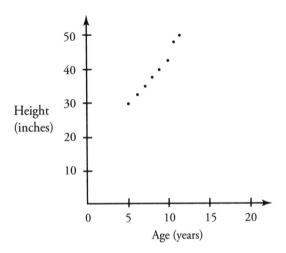

Do this with all of the measurements and then join the points with a line.

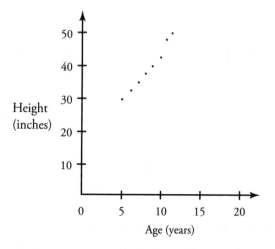

Voila! Your height graph is completed. Show it to your parents if you want to impress them with your incredible growth—their height graphs have probably been flat for years.

READING LINE GRAPHS

Look at the following graph of the number of people in Smalltown who learned to dive over the years 1992 to 2001.

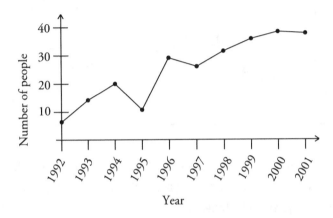

1. How many people in Smalltown learned to dive in 1994?

2. In what year did the greatest number of people learn to dive?

3. In what year did the fewest people learn to dive?

4. Between which 2 years was there the greatest increase in the number of people who learned to dive?

5. Between which 2 years was there the greatest decrease in the number of people who learned to dive?

Sondra pointed a finger toward the bottom of the computer screen. "Let's see what the others have," she prodded. With a click of the mouse, Taylor brought up another window. That article, also from the local paper, had been published in 2001. It also summarized the story of the tunnels and presented the results of a survey taken by the newspaper to find out what people in the city thought of the story.

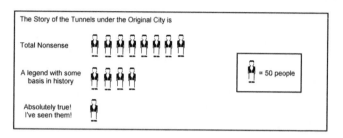

"Not many people believe the story," Taylor said sadly. "Maybe we're on a wild goose chase." Jennifer said nothing and Sondra just nodded, but Mrs. Bridge smiled a little.

"I don't know," she said softly. "There are some eyewitnesses."

○○○○○○○○○○○○

A **pictograph** represents information with little pictures or symbols. For these kinds of graphs, it is important to know exactly what each picture indicates. This is usually done with a key or scale near the graph.

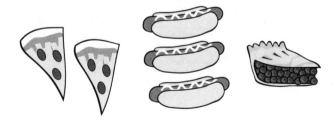

You can make your own pictograph. For instance, you might want to demonstrate where water for swimming is most plentiful in your neighborhood. First, decide on a scale. Here we will use a scale in which each symbol represents 100 gallons. Think of a picture for each location and approximate or figure out how many gallons each water source contains. Here's how it might look if you'd thought of three sources of water: a bathtub, a backyard pool, and a big duck pond.

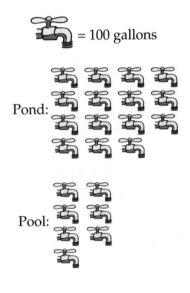

= 100 gallons

Pond:

Pool:

Bathtub:

The legend tells you that each faucet represents 100 gallons of water. By comparing the number of faucets pictured for each location, you get a sense of how much water is in each, and you can compare the sources. By counting the faucets, you can get an approximate number of gallons for each location. Sometimes a pictograph will use only part of a symbol. For example, if each hot dog picture represents 100 hot dogs sold at the ball game, the half hot dog would represent only 50 hot dogs.

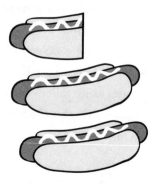

READING PICTOGRAPHS

Look at the following graph of the number of people who listen to music in Smalltown. Each figure represents 100 people.

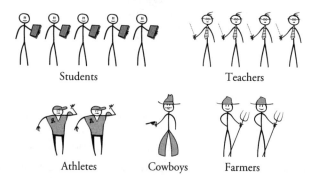

1. How many total farmers in Smalltown like to listen to music?

2. How many teachers in Smalltown like to listen to music?

3. Do more teachers or farmers in Smalltown like to listen to music?

4. In Smalltown, do more athletes or more cowboys like to listen to music?

5. In Smalltown, which group represented has the greatest number of people who like to listen to music?

OOOOOOOOOOOO

Jennifer frowned at the graph on the screen. "Wait! That only adds up to 650 people," she pointed out. "There are more than 650 people in this city. How do we know if these people are typical? Maybe there are more people who believe the story, but they just weren't interviewed."

"That last article may address your concern," Mrs. Bridge said. She turned away and stepped back to her desk. Taylor brought up the window with the third article, which discussed a citywide survey taken in 2005. It included a graph that showed how city residents had responded to a question about the tunnels.

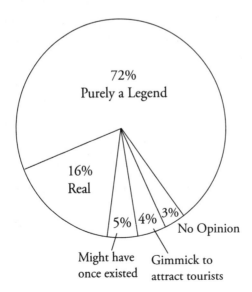

"Well," Sondra said, "almost three quarters of the city thinks the whole story is a fairy tale." She sighed, and Jennifer and Taylor did too.

"So we're part of the 16% that believes the tunnels are real," Taylor said. "We don't have a lot of company."

"No," Jennifer said, "but we do have some company. There are people who believe the story, even some who claim to have seen them. They can't all be crazy." She looked from Taylor to Sondra and back. "Can they?"

OOOOOOOOOOO

A pictograph doesn't always give you a sense of the whole. How many people live in Smalltown, anyway? Well, we don't know. A **circle graph** sees the population of the city as a whole, and represents how that whole is divided. A circle graph, also known as a pie chart, is just like that pizza we were cutting up in Chapter 3, except that the pieces aren't so nice and even. That's why they are represented as percentages. In the circle graph from the newspaper, you can see that 72% of the city residents believe the story about the tunnels is just a myth.

If you know exactly what the whole is, a circle graph can help you figure out the value of each piece of the graph. For instance, let's say that the city has a population of 40,000. If we know that 16% of the residents believe the tunnels exist, then we know that 6400 people agree with Taylor, Sondra, and Jennifer. People often use circle graphs to keep track of budgets, since circle graphs allow you to see relative amounts of a whole very easily.

READING CIRCLE GRAPHS

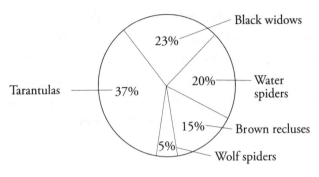

Spider Collection

1. Are there more water spiders or black widow spiders in the collection?

2. Are there more brown recluses or tarantulas in the collection?

3. If there are 100 spiders in the collection, how many spiders in the collection are black widows?

4. If there are 100 spiders in the collection, how many spiders in the collection are water spiders?

5. If there are 100 spiders in the collection, how many of the spiders are *not* tarantulas?

The kids were quiet for a few moments, and then listened to the click, click, click as Taylor closed the windows. One by one, the graphs disappeared from the computer screen. Sondra turned away from the computer and started toward the door. The others followed. They stopped at the desk to thank Mrs. Bridge for her help. "Mrs. Bridge," Sondra asked, "what do you think? Are the people who believe in the tunnels crazy?"

Mrs. Bridge smiled warmly and accepted the piles of books and papers Jennifer and Taylor had retrieved from their table. "I don't know that my opinion—or anyone else's, for that matter—should matter to you. It's what you believe that matters." She sat down in her desk chair and smiled up at the three of them. "You remember that spike in interest you saw in 1975?" The three kids nodded. "One of those people was Mr. Bridge."

Taylor, Sondra, and Jennifer simultaneously crouched to be on eye level with the librarian. "Really?" they asked in unison. Jennifer leaned in, rested her elbows on the desk, and her chin on her hands. "What did he tell you about it?" she asked.

Mrs. Bridge giggled a little. "Not very much, except that he tried, but failed. I'm afraid you'll have to find out more for yourselves."

REVIEW

Look at the following graph of the number of people who could hula hoop in Smalltown.

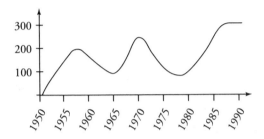

1. Approximately how many people could hula hoop in 1965?

2. Approximately how many people could hula hoop in 1972?

3. What was the year in which the greatest number of people could hula-hoop?

4. Between which 5 years was there the greatest increase in the number of people who could hula hoop?

Sondra created this graph.

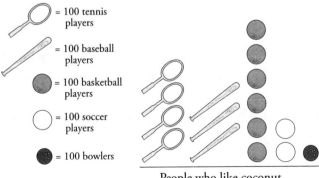

People who like coconut

5. Approximately how many bowlers like coconut?

6. Approximately how many tennis players like coconut?

7. What is the approximate difference between the number of basketball players who like coconut and the number of bowlers who like coconut?

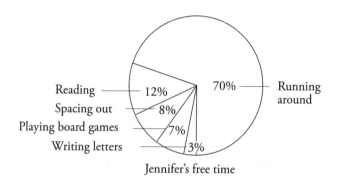

Jennifer's free time

8. Does Jennifer spend more time reading or spacing out in an average week?

9. If Jennifer has 50 hours of free time a week, how much time does she spend reading?

10. If Jennifer has 50 hours of free time per week, how much time does she spend playing board games and writing letters together?

OOOOOOOOOOOO

"OK, the tunnels," said Jennifer said as the kids trotted down the front steps of the museum. "I mean, other people have tried it, right? "

"Tomorrow!" yelled Sondra. "We'll get an early start, but we need to gather up supplies tonight."

"Whoa! What? There's still so much we don't know," said Taylor, as Sondra and Jennifer scampered down the steps. "We don't know how big the tunnels are. We don't know how we prove we've done it, assuming we can do it. We don't even know how to get out. Oh, here we go again."

CHAPTER 8

Geometry

Taylor, Jennifer, and Sondra were up early the next morning. They met on the sidewalk in front of Jennifer's house, each of them carrying a backpack. As they started toward Mr. Ippolitto's shop, they ran down a checklist of supplies. They had bottles of water, snacks, flashlights, pads and pencils, a big ball of string, a roll of tape, and more. Sondra even brought a camera.

"Did you think we were going on vacation?" Taylor teased.

Sondra smiled. "We still don't know how we prove we were there," she said. "At least we'll have some pictures to show for it."

They turned into the alley that led to Mr. Ippolitto's storeroom. At this early hour, there were few people on the street, so they were surprised when they saw an envelope taped to the storeroom door. Jennifer sprinted ahead, saw their names on the front, snatched it up, and opened it.

"It's from Mrs. Bridge," she shouted, then read aloud. "I told Mr. Bridge about the research you were doing in the library and he's excited to hear that you're interested. His attempt at the tunnels wasn't completely successful, but he said you should have this drawing before you start. He wanted me to tell you that he didn't anticipate the depth, but that's all he would say. I'm guessing that you three are going to make a try at the tunnels in the next day or so. I hope you find this note before you do. Ippolitto's seems like a good starting point. Good luck to you. Love, Mrs. Bridge."

Taylor pulled the papers from Jennifer's hands and turned to the second sheet. "It's a drawing," he said, "a diagram, a..."

"A map!" Sondra exclaimed, looking over his shoulder.

"A map?" Taylor looked at her like she was crazy. "It's a bunch of lines."

"Line segments," Sondra corrected.

Jennifer stretched to see over Taylor. "It's just shapes," he said. "It looks like some kind of badge, or magical charm."

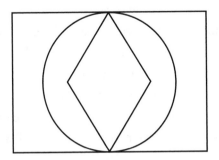

"I think it's Mr. Bridge's attempt to map the tunnels," Sondra insisted, "at least, as much of the tunnels as he got to see."

"Oh. Kay." Taylor stretched the word out and it was clear he wasn't convinced. "How does it help us? Nothing's labeled. We don't even know which end is up."

"What do you want," Jennifer asked, "a big You-Are-Here arrow? We just need to get inside and figure out where on the map we are. Once we have a starting point, we'll be OK."

A starting point is a place. To mathematicians, a **point** is a spot, a location. It *has no dimensions at all*; no height, length, or thickness. A point indicates a place, but, on its own, a point doesn't exist at all. The real world doesn't have objects with no dimensions. A point looks like a dot. If you examined a real-life dot with a microscope, you'd discover that it definitely has dimensions, even thickness. Everything in the real world takes up some space, so there's a sense in which the mathematical idea of a point can only exist in your imagination.

In that imaginary realm, a **line** goes on forever, but has no width or height. You can't draw something that goes on forever, so usually that idea of infinite length is indicated by an arrow at either end, to show that the line just goes and goes and goes. If you were to draw a line with a very sharp pencil, you might say that the line was too thin to measure, thinner than the smallest marks on a ruler. It would still have some small thickness, of course, because it exists in the real world. For mathematicians, though, that line you drew only represents the idea of a line that has no width at all. It is a one-dimensional shape. Here is a line.

A **line segment** has a length you can measure. A line segment is a portion of a line between two endpoints. Like lines, line segments have no width and no height. Here are some segments.

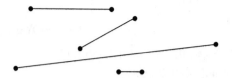

If you see something that looks like a line but only goes forever in one direction, it is a **ray.** Imagine that it's like a ray of sunlight. It begins at a point (the sun) and goes forever in one direction.

An angle, officially, is formed by two rays that have the same initial point. The rays that form the angle are called **sides**, and the point where they meet is called the **vertex**. While the definition says that the angle is made of rays, we still use the word *angle* to describe figures that are formed by two line segments with a common endpoint or the figures that are formed when two lines intersect.

When you measure an angle, you're actually measuring the opening between the sides. Think of the sides of the angle as hands on a clock, with one hand standing still and one rotating. The measurement of the angle is a measurement of how much that side has rotated. Angles are measured in degrees, using an instrument called a **protractor.** A protractor looks like this.

A full rotation, once around the circle, is 360 degrees. To find out how many degrees a specific angle has, line up the bottom of the protractor with one of the sides of the angle, making sure the center of the protractor is at the vertex of the angle. Look to where the other side of the angle falls. The number that side falls over is the measure of the angle. If your protractor has two sets of numbers—and most do—look back to the side you lined up with 0. If you used the 0 on the bottom set of numbers, read the measurement from the bottom set. If your 0 was on the top, read the top numbers.

An **acute** angle is an angle of less than 90°. Acute means sharp, and acute angles have a sharp point. All of these angles are acute.

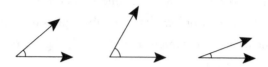

An **obtuse** angle is one greater than 90 degrees. Obtuse means thick, so look for a thick shape when you're looking for an obtuse angle. These angles are all obtuse.

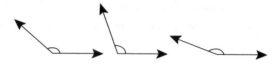

If you pick a point on a line and call it the vertex, a line can be thought of as a **straight angle**. It has exactly 180 degrees, which would be written like this: 180°. The small circle just after the 0 is the degree symbol.

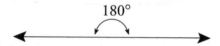

A **right angle** is an angle that is exactly half of the straight angle. That means that right angles are exactly 90°. Right angles are labeled by tiny squares in the vertices.

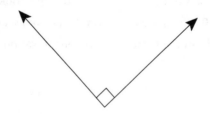

When one line intersects another and divides the straight angle exactly in half, right angles are formed. When two lines meet this way and form right angles, the lines are called **perpendicular.** The symbol for perpendicular is ⊥. Let's see how this looks below.

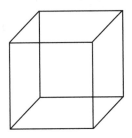

When lines never intersect, they are **parallel.** They stay an equal distance apart, no matter how far they go on. The symbol to show that lines are parallel is this: ‖ .

It's important to remember that just because two line *segments* don't intersect doesn't mean they're parallel. If you want to know if two line segments are parallel, they have to be extended to infinity—that is, turned into *lines.* If they would ever touch when extended, then the line segments are not parallel.

POINTS, LINES, AND ANGLES

Use this figure to answer the questions below.

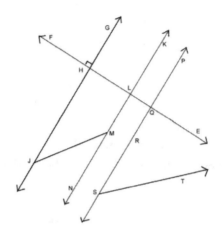

1. Name a line.

2. Name a line segment.

3. Name a ray.

4. What is the vertex of ∠RST?

5. Name its sides.

6. Name an angle that looks acute.

7. Name one that looks obtuse.

8. Which two lines are perpendicular?

9. Name a right angle.

10. Which two lines are parallel?

Sondra turned back to the storeroom door and entered the security code. The buzzer sounded softly, and Taylor pulled the door open, holding it while Sondra and Jennifer passed through. He stepped inside and reached for a small box to prop the door open.

"You can't do that," Sondra reminded him. "Remember? Mr. Ippolitto said if we prop the door the alarm will sound."

"So how is anyone going to know we're in here?" Taylor asked.

"You did talk to your parents, didn't you?" Sondra asked, but didn't wait for an answer. "And we'll leave a note for Mr. Ippolitto," she said, pulling out a pad and pencil. She scribbled a note, then dug out her tape, and fixed the paper to a box at eye level. "Anyone who walks in should see that."

Together the three kids moved the boxes they had stacked in front of the mysterious door and rested for a minute before they tried to open it. It gave on the first try. Jennifer pulled a ball of string out of her backpack, tied one end to the door handle, and stepped through the door. "We're going to need the flashlights," she called back.

"And the insect repellent," Taylor complained. "And the mouse repellent. And the snake repellent. And what's with the string?" he asked as he stepped reluctantly through the door.

"It's a way to tell where we've been, so we don't go around in circles," Sondra explained as she followed him. "And to find our way back if we need it."

"So…" Taylor flipped his flashlight around. "Where are we?"

"I'm not exactly sure," Sondra mumbled. "We don't seem to be at a vertex." She looked first in one direction, then the other. "It doesn't look the way I expected it to."

"Mr. Bridge's map looks like a rectangle, a circle, and a…" Jennifer tipped her head to one side. "A tilted square."

"Well, yes," Sondra said with a shake of her head. "Most people would call it a diamond, but I suppose 'tilted square' will do."

Taylor started to pace. "But Mr. Bridge's map may not be complete. He didn't get all the way through the tunnels. Maybe there are more tunnels than on his map. There could be triangles, trapezoids…"

OOOOOOOOOOOO

Many geometric shapes are made of line segments. Shapes that are made from line segments are called **polygons**. To form line segments into these shapes, you make the endpoints of the line segments meet. The places where line segments meet are the **vertices** (the fancy name for corners). If you are only talking about one corner, it's a **vertex**. At each vertex, an **angle** is formed. The segments connecting the vertices are called **sides**.

These shapes are **planar,** or **two-dimensional**. Both of these terms describe a shape as flat. They are called two-dimensional because they have length and width (2 dimensions) but no thickness.

The way to identify most polygons is to count the number of sides. A polygon with 3 sides is a **triangle.** A triangle with 3 equal sides also has 3 equal angles—acute angles, as you can see in the picture below—and is called an **equilateral triangle.** When a triangle has 2 equal sides, it also has 2 equal angles. A triangle with 2 equal sides is called an **isosceles triangle.** The isosceles triangle that is furthest to the right has a right angle, which means it is not only an isosceles triangle, but also a right triangle. A **right triangle** is a triangle that includes a right angle. A triangle in which all 3 sides are different lengths and all 3 angles are different sizes is a **scalene triangle.**

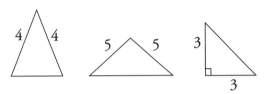

A polygon with 4 sides is a **quadrilateral.** When people think of a figure with 4 sides, they often imagine a special quadrilateral like a rectangle or a square, but not all quadrilaterals are squares, or even rectangles.

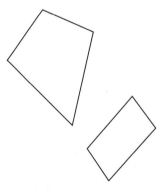

Both squares and rectangles are special kinds of quadrilaterals called parallelograms. A **parallelogram** is a quadrilateral whose opposite sides are parallel. A **rectangle** is a parallelogram that has 4 right angles, and a **square** is a rectangle with 4 sides that are all the same length. A **rhombus** is a parallelogram with 4 equal sides. It can look like a squished square. It has the equal sides like a square, but not the right angles of the rectangle. A square is both a rhombus and a rectangle.

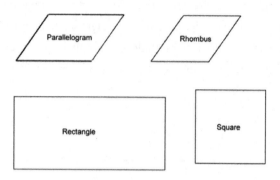

A **trapezoid** is a figure in which 2 of the sides are parallel and 2 are not. It doesn't qualify as a parallelogram because it only has one pair of parallel sides, not 2. It looks a little like a triangle with its top cut off.

Look at the figure below, which is made up of several different polygons, one inside the other. The outside shape is called an **octagon;** *octa-*, as in octopus, means it has 8 sides. The shape just inside it is called a **hexagon;** *hex-* means it has 6 sides. Within that is a **pentagon;** *pent-* means 5, like the Pentagon building that houses the United States Department of Defense. Inside the pentagon is a **quadrilateral;** *quad-*means 4. Notice that none of these shapes requires right angles or equal sides.

If you were to draw a line that went from one corner of a quadrilateral to the opposite corner, such a line would be called a **diagonal.** In polygons with more than 4 vertices, a diagonal is a line segment that connects 2 vertices but isn't a side.

○○○○○○○○○○○○

"There could be all kinds of polygons, but we're not in them," Sondra stated flatly.

"How can you be sure?" Taylor was almost shouting now. "We don't know where we are! We're lost!"

Jennifer folded her arms and glared at him. "Taylor, we're 2 feet from Mr. Ippolitto's storeroom. We're not lost."

"Look down there," Sondra said, shining her flashlight toward the end of the corridor. "See where the tunnel turns? It's a corner, so we're not in a circle, and it looks like a right angle, so we're probably in either the rectangle or Jennifer's tilted square."

Taylor wasn't quite ready to calm down, even if Jennifer was glaring at him. "Just because that's a right angle, that doesn't mean it's a square. It doesn't even mean it's a rectangle. What if it's some weird shape with right angles and obtuse angles and acute angles and..." He stopped, but only because he had run out of angles.

Jennifer stopped glaring at Taylor long enough to look at Sondra. "Is that possible?"

OOOOOOOOOOOO

While it's possible to draw crazy shapes like the one Taylor is imagining, their sides would have to zigzag wildly. The shapes you usually see, the polygons, have very predictable angles.

The 3 angles of any triangle will always add up to 180 degrees. You can convince yourself of this by tearing the corners off a triangle and lining them up with their vertices together. They will always make a straight angle.

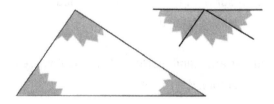

All quadrilaterals have angles adding up to 360 degrees. If you draw a diagonal in any quadrilateral, you make 2 triangles. Look at the drawing below and you can see that the angles of the 2 triangles make up the angles of the quadrilateral. Each triangle contributes 180 degrees to the total, so there are 360 degrees in the quadrilateral.

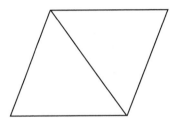

THINK ABOUT THIS

In polygons with more than 4 sides, can you find a rule for what the angles will add up to? Choose 1 vertex and draw all the diagonals you can from there. How many triangles do you get? Each triangle has 180 degrees. How many degrees do all the angles together give you?

Taylor didn't wait for Sondra's reassurance. He had found something else to worry about. "What if there's more than one square? What if there are hundreds of rectangles that all look exactly the same? We'll never know where we are! We'll be lost forever!"

If you see two figures or angles that are the exact same size and shape, they are said to be **congruent**. When you find triangles (or other polygons, for that matter) with identical sides and angles, you know they are called congruent. These two quadrilaterals are congruent.

These two are not.

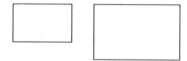

If two triangles have equal angles and sides that are in the same ratio, these triangles are similar. The two triangles below are **similar**. The ratio of the three sides is the same for both triangles. (It's 3 : 4 : 5. Even though the bigger one is labeled 6 : 8 : 10, it is the same ratio as 3 : 4 : 5.)

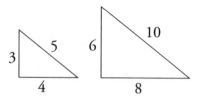

Congruent polygons look like identical copies of one another, but similar polygons look like one is an enlarged version of the other.

"OK, OK, OK!" Sondra realized she was shouting—and realized that the tunnels echoed—so she took a deep breath before she said anything else. "It's true we don't know much about the tunnels, but getting upset isn't going to help. Can we just work with what we do know and not get in a panic?"

Taylor's embarrassment was obvious, and he muttered an apology. Jennifer turned slowly in place. "What exactly do we know?" she asked when she came round to face Sondra again.

Sondra thought for a minute. "Well," she said at last, "we know that this is not the circle."

⭕⭕⭕⭕⭕⭕⭕⭕⭕⭕⭕⭕⭕

A **circle** is defined as all the points that are at a specified distance from a center point. One way to draw a circle is to take a small piece of string and place one end of it in the middle of a sheet of paper. Tie your pencil or pen point to the other end of the string and, while pressing the central end down, run your pencil all the way around it at the greatest length the string will allow. You should end up with a perfect circle. The place where you held the string down is the center point, the length of the string is the specified distance, and the circle you drew is made up of all the points that far from the center.

The **center** of a circle is the point exactly in the middle, so every point of the circle is an equal distance from the center of the circle. While you cannot have a circle without a center, the center is not technically part of the circle. If you draw a line segment from the center to any point on the circle, that segment is called a **radius**. If you draw more than one radius, you have **radii**, not radiuses. The length of that segment is also called the radius, and the radii are all the same length.

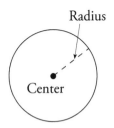

Look at a circle with a line segment drawn through the center. This segment is called a **diameter.** A diameter is a line segment in a circle that goes through the center and has its endpoints on the circle.

Diameter

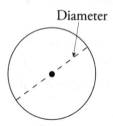

The distance around a circle is called the **circumference,** not the perimeter, and circles have their own special interior ratio. If you measured the circumference of a circle and compared that measurement to its diameter, you would find that the circumference is always a little bit more than 3 times the diameter. The relationship between these 2 measurements—the ratio between them—is called **pi.** It's pronounced "pie," as in blueberry pie. It is a Greek letter, and it looks like this: π. The value of π is approximately 3.14, though the actual exact value goes on forever and ever, an infinite decimal. So, if you know the diameter of a circle and you want to know the circumference, just multiply the diameter by 3.14, and if you know the circumference and you want to know the diameter, just divide the circumference by 3.14.

THINK ABOUT THIS

How many grooves do you think are on the circumference of a dime? Would you believe 118?

POLYGONS AND CIRCLES

Use the drawing to answer the questions below.

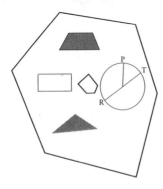

1. Name the largest polygon according to the number of sides.

2. Name the smallest polygon according to the number of sides.

3. The shaded triangle has one angle that measures 31 degrees and one that measures 42 degrees. Find the measurement of the missing angle.

4. Tell whether the shaded triangle is acute, right, or obtuse.

5. The shaded quadrilateral has one angle that measures 60 degrees, a second that is 120 degrees, and a third that is 55 degrees. Find the measurement of the fourth angle.

6. Is the shaded quadrilateral a parallelogram?

7. Are the shaded triangle and the unshaded triangle congruent?

8. Are the two quadrilaterals similar?

9. Name a radius and a diameter of the circle.

10. Find the circumference of a circle with a diameter of 4 centimeters.

○○○○○○○○○○○

Jennifer made another slow turn in place. "What are we getting into?" she wondered aloud. "I mean," she said as she stopped turning and looked at Sondra and Taylor, "do we have any idea how big this tunnel system is? Do we know how long it will take to get through it? Minutes? Hours? Days?"

Taylor looked like he couldn't decide whether to faint or be sick. Sondra swallowed hard and opened her mouth, but nothing came out. Suddenly, she dropped her backpack with a thud, and started rummaging inside it. She pulled out a pad and started flipping through it.

"What are you looking for?" Taylor and Jennifer asked in unison.

"Thirty-six square miles," Sondra cried and stopped flipping. "At the museum yesterday we figured out that the original city was 36 square miles."

"And that helps us how?" Taylor asked.

Sondra pulled out a pencil. "I'm not sure, but I thought we might be able to use it to estimate the size of the tunnel system. If the tunnels were built under the original city, the biggest polygon the tunnels make won't have an area any bigger than 36 square miles." She crouched down and started to work some math on her pad.

"Thirty six square miles?" Taylor shrieked. "Do you know how big that is?"

"No," Jennifer said, "do you?"

"27,878,400 square feet," Sondra said calmly, "or 3,097,600 square yards."

Jennifer and Taylor plopped down on the ground and stared at Sondra in horror.

OOOOOOOOOOOO

What are square feet? They are squares that have sides measuring 1 foot each, and square inches are squares that have sides measuring 1 inch each. These types of square measurements are how people measure flat surfaces. One square foot is the size of a large floor tile or the size of a bandana.

The number of square feet a surface occupies, or the number of square yards of fabric needed to make a tablecloth, or carpet to cover a floor, or... okay, you get the idea; all those things are found by finding the **area** of the shape. Area tells us how many square units—square feet, or inches, or yards, or meters, or miles, or any other unit of distance—a shape occupies.

For any rectangle (including squares), the area is found by multiplying the **length** of the shape by its **width.** The length of a rectangle is its longer side, and the width is its shorter side. Since the rectangle below has length of 4 and a width of 3, the area of that rectangle is 12 (4 × 3 = 12).

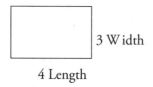

3 Width

4 Length

If a rectangular swimming pool is 50 yards long by 25 yards wide, how many square yards does it cover? It's 50 yards times 25 yards, which is 1,250 square yards. Suppose you wanted to know how many square *feet* there are in the pool. How would you figure that out? A lot of people would multiply the number of square feet by 3 since there are 3 feet in one yard, but that's a common mistake. Look at this drawing:

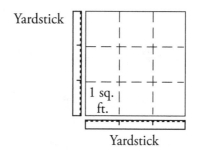

You can see that there are 9 square feet in 1 square yard. A *linear* yard (linear means "along a line") contains 3 linear feet. A *square* yard is 3 feet by 3 feet. It contains 9 square feet.

To figure out how many square feet are in the pool, we should multiply the length of 50 yards times the width of 25 yards, and then, to change that number to square feet, multiply by 9. That's 11,250 square feet! You could also begin by changing 50 yards to 150 feet and 25 yards to 75 feet, and then multiply 150 times 75 to get 11,250 square feet!

To find the area of a square, you also multiply the length times the width. Because all the sides of a square are equal, the length and width are equal. So the same number is multiplied by itself, or one of the sides is squared. (Does it make more sense now why multiplying something times itself is called "squaring"?)

The terms **length** and **width** are sometimes replaced by the **base** and **height.** Some people also call these the **dimensions** of a polygon. The height of any polygon is the length of a segment drawn from its highest point perpendicular to its base. The height must always make a right angle with the base. In the case of the triangle below, for example, the height is measured from the top of the triangle straight down to the imaginary line continued from the base.

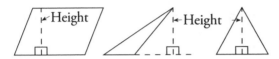

Rectangles and squares are part of a category of quadrilaterals called **parallelograms**. A parallelogram is a quadrilateral in which the opposite sides are parallel. The area of any parallelogram can be found by multiplying the base times the height. This is usually written as $A = bh$. If you cut a triangle off 1 side of a parallelogram and move it around to the other side, you turn the parallelogram into a rectangle, whose area is $A = bh$. The area of the parallelogram below is 18.

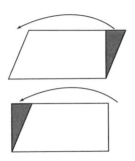

Since two triangles make a parallelogram, we can find the area of a triangle by cutting a parallelogram in half. The area of a triangle is half the area of a parallelogram. The area of a triangle is one-half of the base times the height, also known as $A = \frac{1}{2}bh$. The area of one of the triangles in the figure below is 12, while the area of the whole rectangle is 24. Remember that the height of the triangle must be perpendicular to the base, or it isn't the height.

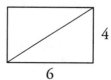

A trapezoid is a bit trickier. The area of a trapezoid is one-half the sum of the parallel sides times the height. The area of the trapezoid below is 55 square units.

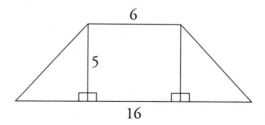

If, instead of finding the area of one of these shapes, you wanted to figure out how many inches of string it would take to wrap its edges, that measure would be called the **perimeter.** The perimeter is the length of the outside border of a shape. To find the perimeter, just add up the sides of a figure.

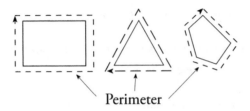

Perimeter

A circle's area can be found by multiplying π by the square of the radius, also known as $A = \pi r^2$. The area of the circle below is 9π.

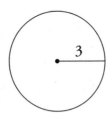

To find the circumference, multiply π times the diameter, or, since the radius is half the diameter, multiply π by the radius times 2. These 2 formulas are written as $C = \pi d$ or $C = 2\pi r$. The circumference of the previous circle is 6π.

PERIMETER AND AREA

1. Find the area of a square with sides 12 meters long.

2. Find the perimeter of the square in Question 1.

3. Find the perimeter of a rectangle that is 18 feet long and 5 feet wide.

4. Find the area of the rectangle in Question 3.

5. Find the area of a triangle with a base of 194 centimeters and a height of 22 centimeters.

6. Find the area of a parallelogram with a base of 9 inches and a height of 4 inches.

7. Find the area and perimeter of a rectangle 14 feet long and 9 feet wide.

8. Find the area of a trapezoid with a height of 10 feet, if the shorter base is 13 feet and the longer base is 19 feet.

9. Find the circumference of a circle with a diameter of 6.5 inches.

10. Find the area of the circle in Question 9.

OOOOOOOOOOOO

Sondra looked up from her pad to see the looks of despair on Jennifer's and Taylor's faces. "Those numbers sound huge, don't they?" she asked. Jennifer and Taylor just nodded. The three kids sat in silence for a few minutes, with numbers in the millions echoing in their heads.

Jennifer perked up first. "You know, I can't even make sense of those numbers. I don't know how to imagine millions of square feet. Let's think about it a different way." She took Sondra's pad and pencil and started to draw.

"Let's suppose that the largest polygon in the tunnel system is a square." She drew a square on the pad. "And let's suppose it has an area as big as the original city—36 square miles. That would mean the side of the square is 6 miles."

"That doesn't sound much better," Sondra said.

"Six miles on each side," Taylor said, "times 4 sides means it could have a perimeter of 24 miles. We can't walk 24 miles."

"We got up early for nothing," Jennifer said sadly.

Sondra frowned. "Are we going to just give up?" Taylor started to nod.

Jennifer looked up. "What choice do we have?"

Sondra stood up and looked around. "Couldn't we just explore this tunnel a little? I mean, we're here. Shouldn't we see something?"

Jennifer got to her feet. "We don't know the tunnels are 6 miles on a side. They might be a lot smaller. That corner's not 6 miles away. And where are the other tunnels in Mr. Bridge's picture? I say we find out."

Taylor looked up at Jennifer, then Sondra. "Oh, all right," he said as he got to his feet. "Which way?"

"Let's pace off the distance to that corner." Jennifer waved her flashlight around to light the distant turn. She started walking, counting her paces as she went. Sondra and Taylor followed. Sondra swept her flashlight over the floor in front of them, and Taylor played out string as they walked.

"We don't have 6 miles of string," Taylor pointed out.

"It's not 6 miles," Sondra said.

Jennifer said nothing until they reached the corner. "880 paces," she announced. "Each of my paces is about a foot and a half, so… where's the pad?"

Sondra was already calculating. "1,320 feet," she announced. "That's about a quarter mile."

"And it is a right angle corner," Taylor observed. "That looks like another one," he said, gesturing to the next turn with his flashlight.

Jennifer started walking again, counting as she went. Taylor and Sondra hurried to keep up. "That's only 660," she said when she reached the turn.

Sondra calculated. "990 feet. So, we're in a rectangle, not a square."

Taylor swept his light over the walls. "Have you noticed any other doors?" he asked. "We've come a ways. Can you figure out where we are now? I mean, what we're under?"

"Well, let's see how far from Mr. Ippolitto's we are." Sondra muttered her way through some multiplication. Jennifer looked over Sondra's shoulder and made a suggestion. "Oh, yeah, that works," Jennifer remarked, then multiplied some more. "We're about 1,650 feet from Mr. Ippolitto's," she announced.

Taylor stopped examining the walls and looked at her. "How do you figure that?"

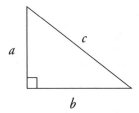

Sondra used the **Pythagorean theorem.** She saw that the tunnels they had paced off would form the legs of a right triangle. The Pythagorean theorem says that for any right triangle, the square of the 2 shorter sides added together will equal the square of the longest side. The longest side, also known as the **hypotenuse,** is the side opposite the right angle. The shorter sides of a right triangle are also known as the **legs.** For a right triangle with legs labeled a and b and hypotenuse c, the formula is $a^2 + b^2 = c^2$.

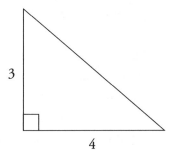

If you had a right triangle with legs of 3 and 4, it would be easy to figure out the third side. Square the length of each leg and add the square of the legs.

$$a^2 + b^2 = 3^2 + 4^2 = 9 + 16 = 25$$

What squared equals 25? Five squared is 25, so the third side is 5.

Since Jennifer paced out the two sections of the tunnel, Sondra could estimate the length in feet. She approximated that the two sections were 990 feet and 1320 feet long. The straight line distance from where they are to Mr. Ippolitto's is the third side of the right triangle.

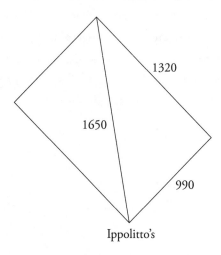

Ippolitto's

It would have taken Sondra a long time to square 990 and square 1,320, and then after she added those squares together, she would have had to figure out what number squared would equal that answer. (2,722,500, in case you were wondering.) That would have taken a very long time.

Instead, Jennifer reminded her of a trick she could use. Jennifer knew that if the legs of a right triangle measure 3 and 4, the hypotenuse would be 5, and she remembered that she had counted 880 paces and 660 paces. $880 = 4 \times 220$ and $660 = 3 \times 220$. Since those numbers were multiples of 3 and 4, Jennifer guessed that 1320 and 990 were multiples of 3 and 4. $1320 = 4 \times 330$ and $990 = 3 \times 330$. Multiples of 3 and 4 as legs will give a multiple of 5 as a hypotenuse. Since the legs are 3×330 and 4×330, the hypotenuse will be 5×330 or 1,650.

THE PYTHAGOREAN THEOREM

Find the hypotenuse of a right triangle whose legs have the measurements given.

1. 5 cm and 12 cm

2. 6 feet and 8 feet

3. 50 inches and 120 inches

4. 30 miles and 40 miles

5. 25 meters and 60 meters

Taylor went back to examining the walls, sweeping his flashlight from floor to ceiling. "So where does 1,650 feet from Mr. Ippolitto's actually put us?" he asked.

"It's about a third of a mile," Jennifer thought out loud. She looked at where they had come and considered directions. "I think we're somewhere on the far side of the museum."

"We should probably move on," Sondra said, pushing the pad and pencil back into her pack.

"Hang on," Taylor said. He pointed his flashlight at the floor by the wall. "Look at this." Jennifer and Sondra looked at the floor where the beam of light fell. Scattered over an area about the size of a school desk were several tarnished coins. Taylor crouched down and picked one up. He turned it over in his fingers a few times. "It says –2."

Sondra picked up another coin. "This one says +3. What do you think they are?" No one had an answer, but the kids agreed to gather the coins up, just in case. When they had gathered up the coins, they set out again to walk the two remaining legs of the tunnel. Taylor kept searching for doors, and since she didn't need to count steps anymore, Jennifer watched the floor and found a few more of the strange coins.

"Uh, what is that?" Jennifer asked as they approached their starting point again. Taylor and Sondra followed the beam of Jennifer's flashlight to spot where the tunnel walls were no longer flat. From where they stood, the kids could see 4 walls of the structure. They guessed that it was in the shape of an octagon, but in 3 dimensions instead of 2. Above a curving metal door in the front wall, a sign said –2. Beside the door was a rectangular metal plate with a round button in the center.

"It sort of looks like an elevator," Taylor said. "Do you think we should push the button?"

Jennifer and Sondra exchanged glances. "I guess it couldn't hurt," Sondra said. Taylor pressed the button and in the distance, they heard a motor hum. In a moment, the door slid open. On the other side, a dimly lit car appeared, just large enough for the three kids to stand inside. It was not octagonal, but circular. The curving walls were dusty, and the round floor and ceiling were about 7 feet apart.

"It's like a giant soup can," Jennifer said.

Taylor looked around. "At least it's a change from these boxy tunnels."

"Do you think it's big enough to hold the three of us?" Sondra asked.

"There was no sign of this on Mr. Bridge's drawing." Jennifer said.

"Mr. Bridge's drawing wasn't three-dimensional," Sondra pointed out.

"He didn't anticipate the depth," Taylor remembered. He looked at Jennifer and Sondra. "I think we just found the elevator."

⬤⬤⬤⬤⬤⬤⬤⬤⬤⬤⬤⬤⬤

The real world is made of **three-dimensional** shapes. The flat surfaces of three-dimensional shapes are called **faces**; the line segments that make up the sides are called **edges**; and the corners, like the corners of other shapes, are called **vertices**. Three-dimensional shapes that are made up of polygons are called polyhedrons. Other three-dimensional figures aren't polyhedrons, so sometimes we just talk about **solids** when we mean all these different three-dimensional figures.

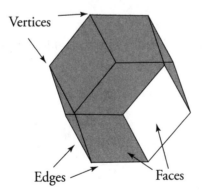

Many of the solids we encounter are made from two identical polygons, floating one above the other, connected by line segments. These are called **prisms**, and are sometimes named for the polygons that form their bases.

A prism that has squares for all six of its faces is called a **cube**. The figure below shows a rectangular prism, a hexagonal prism, and a cylinder. The **cylinder** is similar to a prism, but has circles as its bases, like a can of soup.

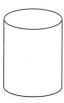

Other solids have a polygon as a base, surrounded by triangles that tip in to meet at a point. These are called **pyramids**. A **cone** is a shape that tapers evenly from a circle down to a single point.

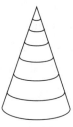

The **sphere** is a solid that doesn't fit into either of those categories, but everyone has seen one. It's a ball.

Three-dimensional figures take up space, or have the possibility of holding material inside them. We talk about the amount of space they take up or the amount of stuff they can hold as **volume**, and we measure volume in cubic units.

Finding the volume of a rectangular solid is a lot like finding the area of a rectangle. The surface of a pool is 25 yards by 50 yards, so its surface area is 1,250 square yards. To find the volume, just multiply those first two dimensions by the third dimension, the depth. This pool is all 3 yards deep.

Volume is length times width times depth, or, $V = l \times w \times d$.

There are 3,750 cubic yards of water in the pool.

3-DIMENSIONAL FIGURES AND VOLUME

1. What is the name of this solid?

2. Name the different solids that make up this figure.

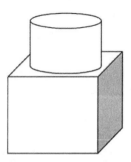

3. Find the volume of a rectangular solid that is 4 feet wide, 9 feet long, and 8 feet high.

4. Taylor has a box to hold jellybeans. The box is 18 inches long, 10 inches wide, and 6 inches high. If 500 cubic inches of jellybeans weigh one pound, how much will the box weigh when it's full of jellybeans?

5. Jennifer has a box 24 inches long, 8 inches wide, and 5 inches high. If she fills her box with jellybeans too, will she have more or less than Taylor? How much more or less?

The kids stepped inside, one by one, and looked around the car. Over the door, a panel showed a series of numbers.

–9   –6   –5   –4   –2   –1   3

The –2 was lit up.

At shoulder level, just beside the door, Taylor found a panel. It had several rows of slots, and under each slot was a little light-up display. Two slots held coins, like the ones they had found in the corridor. Under those slots, the displays showed +1 and –3.

Jennifer reached into Taylor's backpack and pulled out the coins they had collected. "I think we need to learn how to run this thing."

REVIEW

1. What is this shape?

2. What is the name of this shape?

3. What is the line that passes through the center of a circle?

4. Approximately how many degrees are in this angle? Is it obtuse, acute, or right?

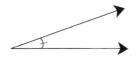

5. What is the volume of this rectangular solid?

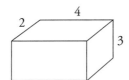

6. Sondra is painting a line around the edge of her carpet. How long will the line be?

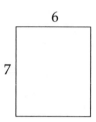

7. Taylor is trying to determine how many right angles are enclosed in this figure. How many are there? (If an angle in this picture looks right, it is right.)

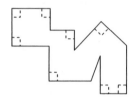

8. Jennifer wants to cut a piece of burlap to cover an ugly picture of a duck that her parents put on the wall of her bedroom. If the picture is a rectangle with a length of 3 feet and a width of 2 feet, how many square feet of burlap will she need?

9. Taylor is trying to describe the shape of a new sculpture his father made to a friend over the phone. The sculpture is shown below. How should he describe it?

10. Sondra is carving a circular tray out of wood for her mother. If the tray is 4 feet across from edge to edge through the center, what is its measurement around the edge?

CHAPTER 9

Negative Numbers

Sondra looked back up at the panel of numbers above the door. The −2 was still lit. She stepped out of the car and looked again at the sign above the door on the outside. It also said −2.

"I think the number up there are supposed to tell us where we are," she said, "but I don't really understand why they're not just regular counting numbers, like other elevators." She pulled out her pad and copied the numbers down: −9, −6, −5, −4, −2, −1, 3.

"Have you ever been in a really tall building that has different elevators for different floors?" Taylor asked. "Each elevator only stops at certain floors. I think maybe this elevator only stops at those floors."

"OK, but what's with the dashes, or minus signs, or whatever they are?" Jennifer asked.

"I think they're meant to tell us that we're below the surface," Taylor suggested.

OOOOOOOOOOOO

Below the surface? Taylor's idea is a common way to think about negative numbers. **Negative numbers** are numbers smaller than 0. Remember the number line?

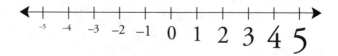

You've already learned about numbers to the right of zero. Numbers larger than zero are called **positive numbers.** Numbers to the left of zero are negative, and the number line extends to infinity in this direction as well.

To think about negative and positive numbers, look at the number line this way.

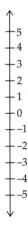

Think of zero as the level of flat ground, and the number line as a ladder dropping into negative numbers. Zero is neither positive nor negative. Think of it as ground level. Up is positive. Down is negative.

The kids are at negative 2, or −2. That would mean that they are 2 levels below ground. If they could go down another 3 levels, where would they be? They would be five levels below ground, or at −5. On the number line it would look like this:

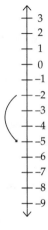

If you look on the number line, you will notice that −5 is below −2. This tells you that −5 is actually smaller than −3. When you think about positive and negative numbers, remember that the sign tells you whether you're above or below 0. Think about the number line or elevators to help you compare them.

Thinking about owing money sometimes helps you understand negative numbers. Would you rather owe someone 3 dollars or 500 dollars? Owing 3 dollars would be better, because it is easier to pay back. Owing money is like having negative money. If you have −3 dollars, you owe 3 dollars, and you're better off than if you have −500 dollars, which means you owe 500 dollars.

When in doubt, remember the number line, the elevator, or the money. Whatever is closer to the surface, or higher up, is bigger.

THINK ABOUT THIS

Negative numbers are usually written with a minus sign in front of them to indicate that they are negative; −5 is negative five. While it's perfectly correct to write positive numbers with a plus sign in front, for example, +3, most of the time we don't write the +. It's assumed that numbers without signs in front of them are positive. This habit probably developed because we learn about positive numbers first, and when we do, we only talk about positive numbers, so it doesn't seem like they need a symbol. When we are introduced to negative numbers, we need a way to distinguish them from the positive, so we put the minus sign in front.

ooooooooooo

Jennifer handed Sondra a couple of coins. "Here, these are the ones that have plus signs, and I have the ones that have minus signs. Now the question is, what do we do with them?"

Taylor frowned. "Well, we're at –2 according to the display up there, but the coins in here say +1 and –3. Neither of them says –2, so I guess you don't just put in the coin with the number of the floor you want."

"What floor do we want?" Jennifer asked. "We don't know where anything is. We don't even know what anything is."

Sondra looked at the display above the door and squinted. "I guess we want to go everywhere," she said. "We have to walk all the tunnels. Do you think we could just experiment?"

Jennifer shrugged. "What's the worst that could happen?"

"Oh please, don't ask that question!" Taylor said, shutting his eyes tightly.

Jennifer elbowed him away from the coin slots. "What do you want to try?" she asked Sondra.

"Well, most of the floors seem to be lower than this one. What if we put one of your negative coins in?"

Jennifer looked back and forth between the coins in her hand and the display over the door. "I have a –4. Do you want to try that?"

"Oh, no!" Taylor whispered. The girls scowled at him.

"Let's see what happens," Sondra said. Jennifer slipped the –4 coin into an empty slot. There was a click, then a hum, and a gentle vibration.

"Oh, no!" Taylor whispered again. With a whoosh, the door slid shut, enclosing the kids in the metal cylinder. Taylor's eyes were still closed. They heard a soft clank, and then the cylinder began to slide downward. The light behind the –2 on the upper panel flickered off, the whir of the machinery slowed, and the light behind the –6 clicked on. There was another whoosh and another clank, and then the door and Taylor's eyes opened.

Adding negative numbers is very similar to adding positive numbers. You just have to remember to include the negative sign.

$$-2 + -4 = -6$$

The kids started at –2 and added another –4 to the coin slots. That took them down 4 more levels. You can look at it on the number line.

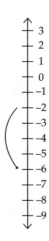

When the signs are the same, combine and keep the sign. That's what you do when you add two positive numbers, isn't it? A positive plus a positive is positive, and a negative plus a negative is negative.

Does that feel like subtraction? Adding a negative number is the same as subtracting a positive. If we wrote $-2 - 4$, that would mean we start at -2 and go further down. Whether we add -4 or subtract $+4$, we're still going down.

OOOOOOOOOOOO

Sondra shone her flashlight into the corridor outside the elevator. Jennifer put one foot out in the corridor, then reached back, and grabbed Taylor's arm to pull him with her. The three kids looked left and right, moving their flashlights slowly over the floor and walls.

"Wow!" Sondra said softly. "This is the circle."

"It doesn't look too big," Taylor said. "Should we try it?"

"Clockwise or counterclockwise?" Jennifer asked, but she started walking without waiting for an answer.

"Keep an eye out for more coins," Sondra reminded them, "or whatever else we might find."

"I still haven't seen another door," Taylor said nervously.

The three kids made the full circle, leaving behind the string they brought to mark the tunnels they had walked. When they arrived back at the elevator, they stopped to have some water and a snack, and Sondra took a few pictures. When they were done, and had made sure that the area was cleaned up, they went back inside the elevator.

"Where to next?" Jennifer asked.

"We have a +2 coin," Sondra said. "If we're right about how this works, that should take us to the –4 level."

"If we're right?" Taylor squeezed his eyes shut again. "What are we doing?" he asked of no one in particular.

Sondra slipped the +2 coin into a slot, and the elevator closed its door again. The car rose slowly, and the door opened again on the –4 level.

⊙⊙⊙⊙⊙⊙⊙⊙⊙⊙⊙⊙

The kids were at –6 and they went up 2. In other words, –6 + 2. Negatives go down, positives go up. What do you think happens? Watch on the number line.

–6 + 2 = –4. In other words, adding a positive 2 to the negative 4 left them higher than they started. They're at –4 instead of –6. Do you remember addition is commutative, that 2 + 3 is the same as 3 + 2? We can change the order when we add positive and negative numbers, too, as long as we're careful with the signs. –6 + +2 can be rewritten as +2 + – 6, or simply 2 – 6. That means from positive 2, go *down* 6 rungs. Watch.

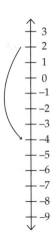

The answer is the same, −4. You get to the exact same place.

Whichever way you think about it, the rule is the same. When the signs are different, find the difference between the numbers and keep the sign of the number that looks bigger. The difference between 6 and 2 is 4, and the 6 looks bigger than the 2, so take the negative sign from the 6. +2 + −6 = 2 − 6 = −4.

We say looks bigger, because of course +2 is bigger than −4. We talk about the **absolute value** of a number, which means the number you would have if you ignored the sign. The absolute value of +5 is 5. The absolute value of −7 is 7. When you add a positive and a negative, find the difference (of the absolute values) and take the sign of the number with the larger absolute value. +12 + −9 = +3, because the +12 has the larger absolute value. +7 + −10 = −3 because the −10 has the larger absolute value.

○○○○○○○○○○○○

Taylor was a little calmer about exploring the −4 level, until he discovered that the level was a triangle. "This isn't on Mr. Bridge's map," he wailed. "We're lost, I tell you, lost!"

"Weren't you the one who said Mr. Bridge's map might not have everything?" Sondra asked. "Just calm down. And look for more coins. We don't have many left."

"Oh, no. Don't tell me that," Taylor said. "What if we can't find the coins we need to get out of here?"

Sondra and Jennifer exchanged glances. "Just calm down," Sondra repeated.

They found 2 more coins as they walked the triangular tunnel. Back at the elevator, they compared their coins to the panel above the door.

"We've been on −2, -6, and now −4. We still have to get to −9, −5, −1, and +3. What coins do we have?" Jennifer asked.

Sondra looked at their collection. "To get to −9, we'd need a −5 coin, which we don't have." Taylor moaned softly. "To get to −5, we need a −1, which…" Taylor moaned again. "To get to −1, we need a +3, and to get to +3, we need a +7." Taylor closed his eyes and tapped his forehead against the wall of the elevator.

"Wait a minute," Jennifer said, "what if…"

"What if what?" Taylor asked, turning to look at the control panel.

"What if we were to take a coin out, instead of putting one in? There's a +1 coin in here. Would taking out a +1 be the same as putting in a −1?" Taylor squeezed his eyes shut again as Jennifer wiggled the coin loose. The elevator closed and started to move. Sondra and Jennifer watched the display above the door, and gave a little cheer when −5 lit up.

The −5 level was not on Mr. Bridge's map either. The kids walked it carefully, and after some confusion at first, they figured out it was a trapezoid. They took extra time to walk it slowly, in the hope of finding more coins, but there were none. Taylor was excited to find a door, but unfortunately, they couldn't open it. That set Taylor back to moaning softly. Sondra added the tunnels they had found to Mr. Bridge's map, and noted the location of the door Taylor had found.

Back at the elevator, Jennifer and Sondra calculated their options. They were on the −5 level, with −1, −9, and +3 still to visit. None of the coins they had could get them to those levels.

"Could we pull something else out?" Sondra asked. Taylor moaned and squeezed his eyes shut tighter.

"Let's see what's left in here," Jennifer mumbled. "There's a −4 coin. What would happen if we pulled that out? Taylor, stop moaning!"

⊙⊙⊙⊙⊙⊙⊙⊙⊙⊙⊙⊙

Jennifer was right to think that subtracting a positive number is the same as adding a negative. $-4 - 1$ give the same result as $-4 + -1$. She wasn't quite as certain about taking away −4, however. Would that be the same as adding 4? Does $-5 - -4$ really equal $-5 + 4$?

Well, what would that mean? To subtract, you go the opposite way. To add a positive, go up. To subtract a positive, go down. You know that when you add a negative, you go down, so when you subtract a negative, go up! A way to remember this is to think of the two negative signs squashing together, forming a plus sign. Two negatives in a row tell you to turn backward, then turn backward again.

NEGATIVE NUMBERS

1. Which is bigger, -5 or -7?

2. Which is bigger, -1 or 0?

3. Which is bigger, -13 or -31?

4. $-3 + -4 =$

5. $-2 + -10 =$

6. $12 + -15 =$

7. $-3 - -4 =$

8. $8 - -10 =$

9. $12 - 17 =$

10. $3 - -2 =$

Pulling out the -4 coin did just what Sondra and Jennifer had guessed (and Taylor had hoped). In a few moments the elevator door opened on the -1 level, and the kids swept the corridor with their flashlights.

"I think we've finally found your tilted square, Jennifer," said Sondra.

Taylor made a face. "It looks an awful lot like all the other tunnels," he said. "Somehow I thought exploring the tunnels would be more exciting."

Jennifer thought about that for a minute. "Yeah, it is sort of strange that it's so... well, dull. I still wonder what they were originally built for. I can't believe someone went to all this trouble just for a challenge."

"I'm starting to get kind of tired," Taylor said.

"And hungry," Jennifer added. "I think maybe we should finish up and get out of here."

"Out of here would be good," Taylor said. "Do you have any idea how we do that?"

Sondra scowled at him, but she realized she was nervous about that too. "Let's finish this tunnel and see where we can go next," she said.

Back at the elevator, they looked at their choices and then at their coins. They were on the −1 level, with the −9 and the +3 still to explore.

"We don't have anything even close to −8," Jennifer said. "We could use a +4 coin to get to +3."

"We've walked almost all the tunnels," Sondra said, "and −9 sounds more like a place for tunnels than +3 does. I'd hate to give up with just one level to go."

Taylor's eyes lit up. "You're saying +3 sounds like the way out, aren't you? I vote for that!"

Taylor and Sondra both looked at Jennifer. "So I have to settle this?" Her friends just stared at her. "OK," she said and looked at the coins in her hand, "I say we go for the −9 level."

"You said we don't have a –8. How are we going to get there?" Taylor protested.

"How about putting –2 coins in 4 times?" Jennifer asked.

You know that when someone says "times," what he is really doing is setting up a multiplication problem. Since Jennifer wants the kids to go down 8 levels, she's suggesting they go down 2 levels 4 times. You can write it this way: $-2 \times 4 = -8$. The rule to remember in multiplication of a negative number is when you multiply a negative number by a positive number, the result will always be negative.

What about a positive times a positive? That's easy. $2 \times 2 = 4$, just like always. A positive times a positive is positive. But what about a negative times a negative? That means going in a negative direction a *negative* amount of times. In other words, the numbers are going backward. It's like saying "not... not," as in "I do not hate Brussels sprouts—*not*." The "nots" cancel out to say, "I do hate Brussels sprouts! " It's the same with negative numbers. A negative times a negative becomes a positive. The rule to remember is that when you multiply a negative number by another negative number, the result will be a positive number.

The trip from the –1 level to the –9 level seemed to take a long time—too long in Taylor's view. This level was a hexagon, a six-sided tunnel. They walked it without talking very much, because they were all feeling a little tired. About half way around, Sondra spoke up.

"What's that?" Sondra asked. She wiggled her flashlight to point out what she had noticed. A small rectangle on the wall at the next turn seemed to be painted in several colors, which made it stand out from the drab grey-brown walls.

Taylor sprinted ahead to see what it was, but Jennifer and Sondra took time to check the tunnel for any signs of coins. They found nothing, and by the time they caught up with Taylor, they were a little worried about that. Taylor held his flashlight at shoulder height to light the message on the wall. Jennifer and Sondra crowded around him to read it as well.

If you've come this far, you've learned a lot.

Can you finish the trip with what you've got?

Complete this circuit, take one more ride,

And look for me when you get outside.

"Look for who?" Taylor asked. "We don't know who did this, or when. This is crazy!"

Sondra spun slowly in a circle, moving her flashlight up and down. "If we could just find out more about why these tunnels were built, we might be able to figure out who built them."

"What's that?" Sondra asked again.

"What's what?" Jennifer asked.

Sondra pointed to a spot on the wall well over their heads. "Am I starting to imagine things, or does it look like there's a sign up there under all the dust?"

"Give me a boost," Jennifer said, and Taylor made his hands into a cradle she could step into. It lifted her just high enough to brush away some of the dust. There was in fact a sign under the dust, and the part they could read said shelter.

"Can we go now?" Taylor asked. The three kids started on the rest of the walk, looking for coins, without luck, as they went. Jennifer and Sondra wondered about what shelter meant, but Taylor just wanted to go home.

Back at the elevator finally, they stopped to do the math. "We're at –9," Jennifer said, "and we need to get to +3. That's 12 levels up."

"We don't have a +12 coin, do we?" Taylor asked.

Sondra looked at her friends nervously. "About all we've got left are some +3 coins."

"How many is some?" Taylor asked.

"We need 4," Jennifer said. She and Sondra counted them out, and in a moment, they were on their way up.

OOOOOOOOOOOO

The problem Jennifer solved so easily was $+12 \div +4 = 3$. Division of positive numbers is a piece of cake. What if one of the numbers was negative? What would be different? The rules for dividing with negative numbers are just like the rules for multiplication. To divide a negative by a positive or a positive by a negative, just divide and keep the negative sign. $+12 \div -4 = -12 \div +4 = -3$. Just like in multiplication, in division if one number is positive and the other is negative, the answer is always negative.

What do you think happens when you divide a negative number by a negative number? How about –12 divided by –4? This yields a positive result, just like multiplying a negative by a negative.

MULTIPLYING AND DIVIDING NEGATIVE NUMBERS

1. $3 \times -4 =$

2. $-22 \times -1 =$

3. $-32 \times -2 =$

4. $-3 \times 0 =$

5. $4 \times -5 =$

6. $-22 \div -1 =$

7. $35 \div -7 =$

8. $-24 \div 6 =$

9. $0 \div -2 =$

10. $-4 \div -2 =$

OOOOOOOOOOOOO

If you're ready, you can try these next problems, which combine everything you have learned so far. If you get confused, try drawing a number line or some kind of visual picture to help yourself out. And don't forget

PEMDAS—the order of operations. Do parentheses first, then do all the multiplication and division, and then combine the positive and negative numbers you're left with.

REVIEW

1. $3 + -4(2 - 1) =$

2. $-5 - 7 + -2 =$

3. $-6 \div -3 \times -2 =$

4. $-1 + 1 + -1 + 1 =$

5. $-2(-3 + -4) - 17 =$

6. $-45 \div -9 + 7 =$

7. $-32 \times 5 \div 2 =$

8. $17 + 23 - -5(2 - 3) =$

9. $35 - 36 =$

10. $35 - -36 =$

OOOOOOOOOOOO

Great job. Check the answers in the back of the book and read the explanations if you have any questions.

CHAPTER 10

Algebra

The final trip in the tunnel elevator was the longest of all, but eventually, the car came to a stop, and the door opened. This time, unlike the others, it opened not on a dark and dusty corridor but on a burst of blinding sunlight and the smell of freshly mowed grass. Taylor held up a hand to shield his eyes from the sun.

"Where are we?" Jennifer asked. Before anyone could answer, the music of a brass band blared out.

Sondra stepped out of the elevator. "Are you kidding? Is this for us?"

"Uh, no," Taylor said. "We've arrived at the Fair Grounds," he said, turning slowly to take in their surroundings, "just in time for band practice."

"There are dozens of people here," Jennifer said, "not including the band. How are we going to find our Mr. X?"

$$\bullet\bullet\bullet\bullet\bullet\bullet\bullet\bullet\bullet\bullet\bullet\bullet\bullet$$

You see, Mr. X can be anyone, and x can be anything—any number. You've probably seen a math problem set up like this: $5 - x = 2$. At first, it may have looked strange. You don't expect letters to pop up in the middle of your arithmetic. But Mr. X is harmless. All x means is some number: x is a **variable.** A variable is just a letter that stands in temporarily for a number that is unknown or changeable. (It doesn't have to be x, by the way. x is only the most common letter used.)

Suppose we say "Let $x = 2$". What else can you figure out? If $x = 2$, then $x + 2$ equals 4 and $x + 7$ equals 9 and $x - 3$ equals -1 (Remember your negative numbers; they're important for algebra.)

How about $2x$? What does that mean? It means 2 times x. You need to get used to the idea that in algebra, when numbers or variables are pressed together with nothing in between, it means to multiply. So if x equals 2, then $2x$ equals 4, because 2 times 2 is 4. When a variable has a number in front of it, such as $2x$, that number is called the **coefficient.** In the example we just gave, 2 is the coefficient of x. If $x = 2$, then $2x$ equals 4 and $3x$ equals 6 and $-7x$ equals -14.

Another way to think of it is that $2x$ means you've got 2 x's $(x + x)$, and $3x$ means you've got 3 x's $(x + x + x)$. You can think of $-7x$ as seven $-x$'s $(-x - x - x - x - x - x - x)$. Remember how addition and multiplication are related? Two times 3 is equal to $2 + 2 + 2$. The rules for math don't change because of the variables. $3x$ (which is x, 3 times) is the same as $x + x + x$. So to add $2x$ to $3x$, you just add the coefficients. $2x + 3x = 5x$. $3x - 6x = -3x$. Got it? Okay, let's try it.

> ### QUIZ #29

ALGEBRA

For questions 1 through 5, let $x = 3$.

1. $x + 1 =$

2. $x - 1 =$

3. $2x =$

4. $2(x) =$

5. $-x =$

For 6 through 8, let $x = -2$.

6. $x - 2$

7. $-3x =$

8. $4x - 6x =$

For 9 and 10, let $x = 12$.

9. $x + 9$, *divided by* 3 $=$

10. $2x - (x + 3) =$

OOOOOOOOOOOO

"Let's think about this logically," Sondra said. "We just eliminate anyone who can't be Mr. X, and see who's left."

"Do you really think there's anyone here for us to find?" Taylor asked. "This mystery person probably forgot all about these tunnels years ago!"

"Well, I think we can eliminate the band," Jennifer said. "That seriously reduces the number of people."

Taylor pointed to a dozen young children who were playing tag. "They're too young to even know about the tunnels," he said, "so we can eliminate them."

"And that just leaves us with…" Sondra looked around the Fair Grounds. "…about a half dozen adults."

"But which one is Mr. X," Jennifer asked. "We haven't a clue."

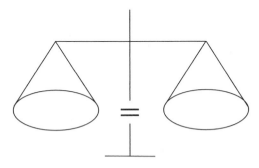

This is where Mr. X really comes into his own. When you don't know exactly what you're looking for, *x* comes in handy.

The key to using *x* is the equal sign. You're used to seeing math problems like this.

$$2 + 3 = ?$$

$$6 \text{ divided by } 2 = ?$$

$$56 \times 2 = ?$$

Because you're used to seeing equal signs with nothing after them—equal signs just hanging out waiting for an answer—it's easy to think that an equal sign is some kind of strange mathematical question mark. It *isn't.* An equal sign means you're looking at an **equation.** An equation means the numbers on either side of the equals sign are perfectly balanced. Get used to thinking of an equal sign as a balance.

When you are doing algebra, working with variables, always think of an equation as a balance. If you do, you'll be able to solve problems like this one.

$$x = 4 - 3$$

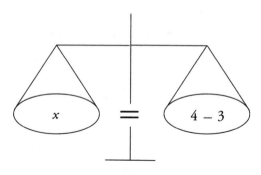

So $x = 1$, or $1 = 4 - 3$, or $1 = 1$.

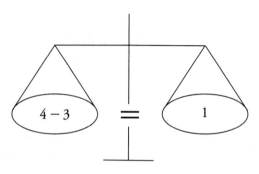

Now try this one.

$$x + 3 = 4$$

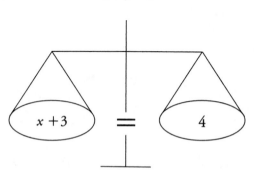

Right now, *x* is unknown. We want to solve for the unknown, also known as solving for the variable. All that means is that you are trying to figure out what number *x* is. The way to figure this out is by **isolating the variable.** That means getting the letter (we're using *x*) all alone on 1 side of the equation, and all the regular numbers on the other side. How?

Think about what has happened to *x*. According to the equation, someone took *x* and added 3 to it, and got an answer of 4. You want to work backwards to find out what *x* was in the beginning. You need to undo what has been done to *x*. Someone added 3 to *x*, so you want to do the opposite: subtract 3.

Like this.

$$17 + 34 = 51$$

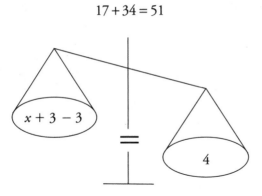

If you just subtract 3 on the left side of the equation, the 2 sides won't be equal anymore. We took away the 3 to get the *x* alone. (The *x* is alone because the 3 and the −3 cancel out.) To keep the balance you need to take away 3 from the other side as well.

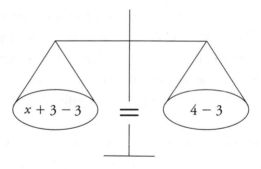

Now it's balanced. Here's the rule to follow when you're doing algebra: Whatever you do to one side of the equation, you must do to the other.

Here's what the problem we tried looks like now.

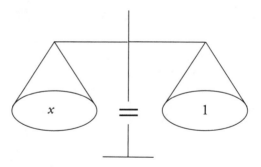

That's it. That's the answer: x equals 1.

Let's try another.

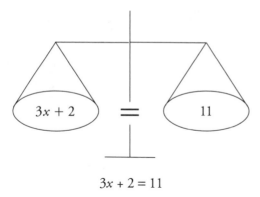

$$3x + 2 = 11$$

What do we do? Isolate the variable, by always doing the same thing to both sides. Someone took x, multiplied it by 3, and added 2. The answer was 11. You need to undo all that.

First, subtract 2 from each side.

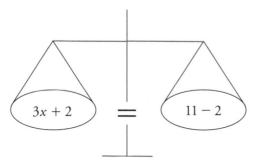

Okay, what's left?

$3x = 9$. Now what do we do? Because x is multiplied by 3, we need to undo that. We need to know what just one x is, so we divide $3x$ by 3. Let's write it out the long way.

$$3 \cdot x \div 3$$

Another way to look at it is

$$51 - 22 = 29$$

Cancel the threes, and you get x by itself. Don't forget to divide the other side. Nine divided by 3 is 3. Here's what our equation looks like now. *Voila!*

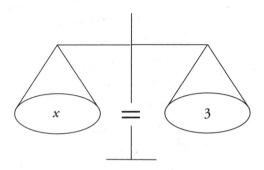

$x = 3$. Great! But what if we had decided to divide by 3 first, and then subtract?

$$3x + 2 = 11$$

If we tried to divide first, we would have to divide both sides of the equation by 3 like this.

$$100 \times 3 = 300$$

Does that look harder? It should, because it is. It's not illegal. You won't get the wrong answer working this way, but you may get frustrated. There's an order to follow in solving an algebra problem, and it's quite simple.

First, combine everything that can be combined. Second, do all the addition and/or subtraction. Third, do the division and the multiplication. If that sounds like the opposite of the order of operations, it is. Remember that the order of operations is the rule you follow when you're doing arithmetic. When you're solving an equation, you're undoing, so the rules are reversed.

Let's try a problem that needs the first and second guidelines and some of the third. (We'll look at rule 3 more carefully in another example.)

$$2x + 3 - 3x + 5 = 17$$

First, combine like terms. You can't combine $2x$ and 3, nor can you combine $-3x$ and 5. *Never try to combine (add or subtract) a normal number and a variable.* In this problem, you should combine $2x$ and $-3x$. What is $2x - 3x$? It equals $-x$. (Technically, it equals $-1x$, but you don't need to write the 1. $-x$ is assumed to mean $-1x$, just as 1 is understood to be the coefficient of x.) Now combine 3 and 5. That's easy, 8. Okay, let's look at what we've got.

$$-x + 8 = 17$$

Subtract 8 from both sides.

$$505 - 300 = 205$$

$-x = 9$. Are you done? Nope. How do we get rid of that pesky negative sign? Easy. Remember that $-x$ means $-1x$, so divide by -1. What's $-1x$ divided by -1? A negative divided by a negative is a positive. One divided by 1 is 1.

$$2 + 0 + 5 = 7$$

Remember to do the same thing to both sides. A positive divided by a negative equals a negative. Nine divided by 1 is 9, so the answer is –9. Did you notice what happens when you divide by –1? All that changes is the sign, which flips. A positive becomes a negative, and a negative becomes a positive. Here's what our problem looks like now.

$$x = -9$$

Are we finished *now*? Yep.

Let's do one more.

$$20 \times 3 = 60$$

First, is there anything to combine? Nope. Is there anything to add or subtract? Subtract 2 from both sides.

$$60 \div 4 = 15$$

Now we have $3x$ divided by 2. How on earth do we undo that? Simple! The x is being divided by 2, so *multiply* both sides by 2.

$$15 + 23 - 17 + 83 = 104$$

You can take it from here, right? Divide both sides by 3, and $x = 10$

OOOOOOOOOOOO

The half dozen adults began to dwindle when 2 of them approached Sondra, Jennifer and Taylor and asked for directions.

"Nice people," Jennifer said when the couple walked away.

"But they're tourists," Taylor pointed out. "They can't be Mr. X."

Sondra thought for a moment. "Do you remember the graphs we saw? Some people think the tunnel legend was meant to attract tourists."

"Oh, good," Taylor said mockingly. "We can give tours."

"There are 4 people left," Jennifer said. "Oh! That's my Aunt Beatrice," she said with surprise. "I don't think she's the mystery person."

"That leaves 3," Sondra said, but just then one of the remaining people called out to the children the kids had already eliminated. The children gathered round the man, then lined up 2 by 2. The man and the woman beside him led the group of children off the Fair Grounds.

"And then there was 1," Sondra said. The single adult left on the Fair Grounds sat on a bench with his back to the kids. They approached the man cautiously, but jumped when he greeted them.

"So, you found your way through the tunnels," Mr. Ippolitto said. "Thank you for leaving me a note. Did you think to draw a map?"

Sondra held out the paper on which they had added more tunnels to Mr. Bridge's map.

"You're Mr. X?" Jennifer asked in amazement, but Mr. Ippolitto just laughed.

"The most recent one, at least, yes," Mr. Ippolitto said. "You've done a good job on the map. I see you found the other door. And obviously, you figured out how to run the elevator. Did you also figure out why the tunnels were built?"

"Something about shelter," Taylor said, "but frankly, it wasn't nearly as exciting as we thought it would be."

Mr. Ippolitto nodded. "I know, I know," he repeated softly. "The legend sounds so exciting, but really it was just developed to try to keep the tunnels from being forgotten. They were built as shelters, emergency shelters. We've never had an emergency big enough to need them, and well, you know, when something isn't used, people forget about it. Sort of like your math skills over summer vacation," he teased.

"But now," he said as he stood up, "you know about them. So now your job is to make sure that the people who come after you don't forget about them."

"How do we do that?" Jennifer asked.

"Oh, you're imaginative," Mr. Ippolitto assured her. "I'm sure you'll find a way. And you're responsible, so I know you'll do your job. You'd feel guilty about collecting your salary if you didn't."

"We get paid?" Taylor asked in amazement.

"I'm afraid it's just a dollar-a-year job, so you won't get rich, and I'm not rich either, so I need to get back to work." He started toward his shop, leaving the three kids confused and amazed on the Fair Grounds. "Oh, by the way," Mr. Ippolitto called back, "your salary also includes free pizza for life."

Sondra and Taylor felt a rush like a sudden breeze, then saw Jennifer running after the man. "Mr. Ippolitto! Wait for me! I'm so hungry!" Jennifer cried.

Taylor and Sondra looked at each other, then at Jennifer and Mr. Ippolitto. "What do you say?" Sondra asked. "Are you hungry?"

"I guess," Taylor said as they started to walk. "You know, those tunnels are really boring."

"I know, sorry," Sondra said.

"I bet we could find a way to make them more exciting," Taylor said.

"You think?" Sondra started to giggle and Taylor laughed out loud. They shifted their backpacks and started to run. By the time they caught up to their friends, Taylor was describing his ideas for the tunnels.

QUIZ #30

EQUATIONS

1. $x + 3 = 7$

2. $x - 9 = 1$

3. $3x = 12$

4. $-3x = -12$

5. $x + 2 + x = 4$

6. $3x + 7 - x = 13$

7. $\dfrac{3x}{2} = 18$

8. $\dfrac{20}{x} = 10$

9. $\dfrac{7}{2x} + 4 = 18$

10. $\dfrac{9x}{3} + \dfrac{2x}{3} = 11$

CHAPTER 11

Review Appendix

WHOLE NUMBERS

This section is designed to help you brush up on addition, subtraction, multiplication, and division with whole numbers. What are whole numbers? Whole numbers have no fractions or decimals and are not negative. Whole numbers are what you probably think of as "normal" numbers. If you made a list of whole numbers, you would start with 0, 1, 2, 3, 4, 5, 6, and go on forever. If you were to take all the whole numbers and also include their negatives, like −1, −2, −3, −4 and so on, you'd have what mathematicians call the integers. So the fancy name for the whole numbers is non-negative integers.

As long as we're on the subject of terminology (**Terminology** is a fancy word for "the names of things."), here's a checklist of terms you should already know but that are covered in this review.

borrowing	quotient	parentheses
factors	digits	sum
product	odd	even
carrying	remainder	primes
multiply	division	times

If any of these words are unfamiliar to you, look for the boldface of that term in the glossary.

ADDITION

Here's an addition problem: What is 12 plus 7? How would you write it out? 12 + 7 = ? There's another way to write it too.

$$\begin{array}{r} 12 \\ +7 \\ \hline 19 \end{array}$$

Especially when you use bigger numbers, you'll find it helpful to stack. Look at what we call place value, or the digit places of a number. A **digit** is one of the numbers 0 through 9. A one-digit number, such as 5, is a number that only has—you guessed it—1 digit. A two-digit number has 2 digits. Examples are 23 or 15. These numbers are made up of two digits. How about 13? That's right; it's a two-digit number. How about 22? That's right; it's also a two-digit number.

The places of the digits matter. You certainly know that 13 and 31 are different numbers, even though they use the same digits. In the number 13, the 3 is in the ones, or units, digit place (either ones or units is okay). The 1 is in the tens digit place.

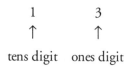

That means the number 13 is made up of three 1s and one 10. 1 + 1+ 1 + 10 = 13. In the number 31, the 3 is in the tens place and the 1 is in the ones place, so there are 3 tens and 1 one. 10 + 10 + 10 + 1 = 31.

Bigger numbers work this way too. Think of 145. The ones digit is 5, the tens digit is 4, and the hundreds digit is 1. So 145 is made up of five ones (5), four tens (40), and one hundred (100).

When you stack numbers to add them, you line them up by their digits places to make sure that you add the ones place to the ones place, the tens place to the tens place, and so on.

Suppose you had to add 19 to 13. First, you would stack the numbers, lining them up by their digit places.

$$\begin{array}{r} 19 \\ 13 \\ \hline \end{array}$$

First add the 9 and the 3 in the ones place. What happens? You get 12. Just look on the number line.

Now think about 12 for a second. It has a 2 in the ones place and a 1 in the tens place. Put the 2 in the ones place of your sum, (A sum is the answer to an addition problem.) and add the 1 to the tens place of the other tens. You now have three ones in the tens place, so put a 3 in the tens place of your sum.

$$\begin{array}{r} {}^{1}19 \\ + 13 \\ \hline 32 \end{array}$$

Of course you can add with the number line as well, but this method of moving the numbers to the next digits place, called **carrying** by mathematicians, will be the easier method to use as the numbers get bigger. Try to imagine adding 199 to 73 using the number line. What a pain!

If you think you can handle the carrying, try this problem: What is 100 + 125 + 95 + 75 + 75? It's an addition problem, and the best way to handle it is to write it on paper and to stack the numbers.

$$
\begin{array}{r}
100 \\
125 \\
95 \\
75 \\
+75 \\
\hline
\end{array}
$$

How much is that? To find out, add up each digit place and carry the numbers again.

$$
\begin{array}{r}
{\scriptstyle 2\;2} \\
100 \\
125 \\
95 \\
75 \\
+75 \\
\hline
470
\end{array}
$$

Did you get the same answer? If not, check your work. Did the units digit place add up to 20? Yes, so you left a 0 and carried the 2. Did the tens place add up to 27? Yes, so you left the 7 and carried the 2. Did the hundreds place add up to 4? Yup. Always be careful to check your work. Checking takes time, but getting the right answer is worth it.

What if the numbers were in a different order; for instance, 100 + 95 + 75 + 125 + 75? Does it make any difference when you add? Nope, you still get 470. Adding the numbers in a different order doesn't make any difference in your answer. No matter how you order the numbers in an addition problem, they will always give the same sum.

Mathematicians have a name for this fact. They call it the **commutative law of addition**. It says something that sounds totally obvious: that $3 + 5$ is the same as $5 + 3$ (or whatever numbers you want to add). But imagine how much more difficult addition would be if that weren't true! If you had to learn what $3 + 5$ was, and then learn what $5 + 3$ was, and if you always had to worry about which was which it would be much harder to do arithmetic. Luckily, you don't have to worry because the commutative property of addition assures you that the sum will be the same no matter what order you put the numbers in.

That's why people will sometimes change the order of the numbers in an addition problem to put numbers that are easy to add next to each other. In $100 + 125 + 95 + 75 + 75$, for example, some people might rearrange to put a 75 right after the 125 because they know that makes 200.

$$100 + 125 + 95 + 75 + 75 =$$
$$100 + \underbrace{125 + 75}_{200} + 95 + 75 =$$
$$\underbrace{100 + 200}_{300} + 95 + 75 =$$
$$300 + 95 + 75 =$$

That leaves adding 95 and 75 as the only hard work, and there's even a trick you can use there. Break the 75 up as $5 + 70$.

$$300 + 95 + 75 =$$
$$300 + \underbrace{95 + 5}_{100} + 70 =$$
$$300 + 100 + 70 = 470$$

Rearranging the numbers to bring together numbers that are easy to add is called looking for compatible numbers.

In the problem above we changed the order of the numbers to bring compatible numbers together, and we worked mostly left to right, but we did do a little bit of jumping over the first number. We can add groups of numbers from an addition problem and then add the answers of those groups to get the final sum. Suppose you had to add $3 + 9 + 7 + 6 + 4 + 5 + 1 + 5$. You could add them in the order given, one at a time, and you'd get the right answer, but a better way would be to group together numbers that add up to 10. Pairs of numbers that add to 10 are compatible numbers.

Here's the "official" way you would do that. First, change the order so that the numbers that add to 10 are next to each other. (That's the commutative property.)

$$3 + 9 + 7 + 6 + 4 + 5 + 1 + 5 = 3 + 7 + 9 + 1 + 6 + 4 + 5 + 5$$

Next, group the pairs of numbers.

$$3 + 7 + 9 + 1 + 6 + 4 + 5 + 5 = (3 + 7) + (9 + 1) + (6 + 4) + (5 + 5)$$

3	9	6	5
+7	+1	+4	+5
10	10	10	10

Now count up the tens. Four tens.

$$(3 + 7) + (9 + 1) + (6 + 4) + (5 + 5) = 10 + 10 + 10 + 10 = 40$$

Forty. Pretty easy, huh? Officially, you used two properties here. The commutative property said we could change the order, and the associative property said we could change the grouping. The **associative law of addition** says that $(4 + 5) + 3$ is the same as $4 + (5 + 3)$. It tells you that when you add a whole bunch of numbers, you can start with any two you want.

By the way, those **parentheses** ( ) surrounding the numbers tell you which part of the math problem should be done first. Because this problem is *all* addition, the parentheses don't matter, but if some of the operations were multiplication or division, the parentheses would be very important.

QUIZ A

ADDITION REVIEW

1. $15 + 29 =$

2. $11 + 23 =$

3. $219 + 393 =$

4. $313 + 32 + 54 =$

5. $4,113 + 332 + 19 + 193 =$

6. Sondra's cat had 13 kittens, and Taylor's cat had 22 kittens. How many kittens do they have altogether?

7. Taylor has 28 race cars, and Jennifer has 113 race cars. How many cars do they have altogether?

8. In the first month of school last year, Sondra missed 2 days. In the third month of school, Sondra missed 17 days (she had her appendix taken out). In the last month of school, Sondra missed 9 days. If Sondra missed no other days of school last year, how many days did she miss in total?

9. Taylor has a stamp collection with only Canadian, English, and Australian stamps. If he has 32 Canadian stamps, 49 English stamps, and 67 Australian stamps, how many stamps does he have in his collection altogether?

10. All the kids went to the seashore this summer. Rose brought back 12 shells, Lionel brought back 31 shells, Sondra brought back 17 shells, Taylor brought back 263 shells, and Jennifer didn't bring back any shells because she was busy riding the waves. How many shells did they bring back altogether?

SUBTRACTION

Subtraction can be thought of as the opposite of addition. When reviewing addition, you learned about carrying. To do subtraction, you'll need to know about something called **borrowing**. In the same way that subtraction is the opposite of addition, borrowing is the opposite of carrying.

Take a look at this problem: $24 - 5$. Twenty-four is larger than 5, but to figure out the digits place you need to subtract 5 from 4. How? Well, if you didn't have enough flour to bake a loaf of bread you might borrow some from your next-door neighbor. Numbers do the same thing. They borrow from their neighbors. In the problem $24 - 5$, the 4 "borrows" a ten from the tens place. There were originally 2 tens, so the ones place can borrow a ten and there will still be 1 left. The borrowed ten, changed to 10 ones, and added to the 4 ones we had, makes 14. Now subtract 5 from 14 instead of from 4, and you will still have a 1 left in the tens place.

$$
\begin{array}{r}
^1\cancel{2}\,^14 \\
-5 \\
\hline
19
\end{array}
$$

A shortcut you can use to make subtraction easier is to subtract numbers in parts. For example, the number 5 can be thought of as (4+1). So instead of 24 − 5, the question can also be thought of as 24 − (4 + 1). Then you can think of it as 24 − 4, which is 20, and then 20 − 1, which is 19. This is especially useful when you need to subtract numbers in your head.

You can also borrow with bigger numbers. How about 101 − 37? Well, 1 minus 7 doesn't work, so you want to borrow from the tens place. Unfortunately, there is only a 0 there, meaning no tens. Don't give up. You have to look to the hundreds place. There's 1 hundred. If the tens place borrows that 1 hundred and changes it into 10 tens, instead of a 0 in the tens place, there will be a 10. The ones place can borrow 1 ten, leaving 9 tens, and you'll have 11 ones. Well, 11 − 7 is 4, and 9 − 3 = 6.

$$
\begin{array}{r} 101 \\ -37 \\ \hline \end{array}
\Rightarrow
\begin{array}{r} {}^{9}\cancel{10}\,{}^{1}1 \\ -37 \\ \hline 64 \end{array}
$$

Here's another kind of problem. Let's say we have 2 cookies and you have 19. How many more cookies do you have than we do? The way to figure out this question is by subtraction. Whenever you want to know *how much more* someone has, subtract. It is easiest to write this question as 19 − 2. Well, 19 − 2 = 17, so you have 17 more cookies than we do.

A way to check your subtraction is with addition. (Remember, subtraction is the opposite of addition.) Does 2 + 17 = 19? It does.

What about a problem like this: You start with 12 cookies, but then you eat 2 and give away 3 to friends. How many would you have left? The easiest thing to do is to subtract numbers one at a time. For example: 12 cookies − 2 cookies = 10, then 10 cookies − 3 cookies = 7. Don't stack more than two numbers in a subtraction problem. But, no matter what, you can always go to the number line if you run into trouble.

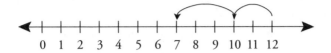

Sometimes subtracting gets a little long for the number line, though. Then you may have to use some other techniques.

SUBTRACTION REVIEW

1. 27 – 12 =

2. 57 – 24 =

3. 131 – 19 =

4. 134 – 29 =

5. 1,001 – 107 =

6. Jennifer has 39 tissues. If she gives 25 of them to Taylor, how many does she have left?

7. Taylor took 23 hamburgers to the barbecue, ate some of them, but then had to take twelve back home without eating them because he overestimated his appetite. How many hamburgers did Taylor eat?

8. Taylor has 225 marbles and Sondra has 132 marbles. How many more marbles does Taylor have than Sondra?

9. Taylor had 117 plastic planes. If 39 of them melted in the sun, how many did he have left?

10. Jennifer has read 1,012 books. If 40 of these are science books and 100 of them are detective novels, how many of them are neither science books nor detective novels?

MULTIPLICATION

Multiplication is related to addition. Suppose you had to add five numbers. If the five numbers were all different, you'd have no choice but to add them, but if you had to add the same number five times in a row, there's a shorter way. The method is multiplication.

Let's take 3 + 3 + 3 + 3 + 3. We're adding the same number, 3, a bunch of times in a row. So instead of adding, we can **multiply**. Multiplication is used to make life a little bit easier. Instead of adding the 3 five times, you say, "three multiplied by five." Another way to say the same thing is to say, "three **times** five." That makes sense, doesn't it? Because you are adding the 3 five *times*. Multiplication can look like any of these.

$$3 \times 5$$

$$3 \cdot 5$$

$$(3)(5)$$

$$3(5)$$

Of course, the result of 3×5 is the same as that of 3 + 3 + 3 + 3 + 3. Both of these operations equal 15. Some cool things about multiplication are

- Any number times 0 is equal to 0.

For example,

$$23 \times 0 = 0$$
$$742 \times 0 = 0$$
$$5,173,294,756,210 \times 0 = 0$$

- Any number times 1 is equal to itself.

For example,

$$15 \times 1 = 15$$
$$2 \times 1 = 2$$
$$16,000,000,000 \times 1 = 16,000,000,000$$

When you add, the result is called the **sum**. So $3 + 3 + 3 + 3 + 3$ gives a sum of 15. When you multiply, the result is called the **product**. So 3×5 gives a product of 15.

Let's try another multiplication problem. Suppose you have five friends and you want to give each of them four presents (because you're generous and kind, or else because you're going to ask them later to do you a really big favor). This problem could be set up as $4 + 4 + 4 + 4 + 4$, but at this point we hope you'd say to yourself, "Let's see, that's four presents five times," and then set it up as 4×5. Excellent: $4 \times 5 = 20$.

An interesting thing about multiplication is that it works in both directions. For instance, you could have said, "Let's see, that's five friends four times…$5 \times 4 = 20$" (which is the same as saying $5 + 5 + 5 + 5$). Being able to switch the order of the numbers is called the **commutative law of multiplication**. Remember the commutative property of addition? This is the same idea, but for multiplication. There's also an **associative law for**

multiplication, which says you can group the numbers in different ways without changing the answer. Here is an easy way to see how these rules work. Here are 20 friends.

Circle them in groups. You can make 4 groups of five friends each, right?

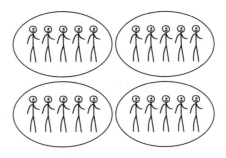

Now here is the same diagram. Try to circle 5 groups of four friends each. That's easy, too, right?

That's how the commutative law of multiplication works.

Multiplication will make many of your calculations much faster and easier, but you have some work to do first. You have to memorize the multiplication table. That way the instant someone says, "What is 4 × 5?" you will know that the answer is 20.

TIMES TABLE

×												
1	2	3	4	5	6	7	8	9	10	11	12
2	4	6	8	10	12	14	16	18	20	22	24
3	6	9	12	15	18	21	24	27	30	33	36
4	8	12	16	20	24	28	32	36	40	44	48
5	10	15	20	25	30	35	40	45	50	55	60
6	12	18	24	30	36	42	48	54	60	66	72
7	14	21	28	35	42	49	56	63	70	77	84
8	16	24	32	40	48	56	64	72	80	88	96
9	18	27	36	45	54	63	72	81	90	99	108
10	20	30	40	50	60	70	80	90	100	110	120
11	22	33	44	55	66	77	88	99	110	121	123
12	24	36	48	60	72	84	96	108	120	123	144

Whenever you get a chance, study your times table. Soon you won't even have to look; you'll know them all. There are some wonderful things about the times table. For instance, look at the nines column. All of the numbers in this column are mirrors of each other, 09 and 90, 18 and 81, 27 and 72. Amazing, right? All those numbers are 9 times something: 9 times 2, 9 times 3, and so on. These numbers—81, 18, 27, and so on—are all multiples of 9. **Multiples** are all the possible products of a number. Now look at the fives column of the times table. Here's something to notice:

All the multiples of 5 on the times table end in 5 or 0. That's because *all* multiples of 5 end in 5 or 0. Even 5 times 1,000,000,000,003 must end in a 5 or a 0. (By looking at the times table, can you guess which one it ends in? It ends in a 5, just like 5 × 3 does.) Think about this, too: When you are multiplying a number by 10, just put a 0 at the end of the number you are multiplying; for example, 10 × 4 = 40. What is 10 × 5? Just add a 0. It's 50.

Do you think there's a shortcut to multiply by 100? Any guesses? To multiply by 100, put 2 zeroes at the end of the number; for example, 4 × 100 = 400. What's 5 × 100? That's right, it's 500.

You might even take a guess about how many zeroes you add when you multiply by 1,000. Well, how many zeroes after the 1? That's right, three, and that's how many zeroes you add. It keeps working like this with all multiples of 10.

What will happen if you multiply by 1? Well, if you have one box of five cookies, how many cookies? 1 × 5 = 5. One times any number is that number.

Here's another term that you should know: **factors**. Whole numbers that multiply to form a product are called factors. For example, 5 × 2 is 10, so 5 and 2 are factors of 10. One and 10 also multiply to form 10, so 1 and 10 are factors of 10. Do any other whole numbers multiply to form 10? (Remember, just whole numbers; we're not counting.) No, 10 has only four factors: 1 and 10, and 2 and 5.

What are the factors of 12? First, you start with 1 and 12. When listing factors of a number, it is best to start with 1 and the number itself, and then to go to the number's next factor that is larger than 1. So the factors of 12 are 1 and 12, 2 and 6, and 3 and 4. The number 12 has six factors: 1, 2, 3, 4, 6, and 12.

What factors can you find for the number 13? Well, first you have 1 and 13, but then what? Look at your times table; do any numbers there multiply to form 13? Nope. That's because 13 has only two factors, 1 and itself. A number with only two factors is a **prime number**. Mathematicians think prime numbers are cool, and they love to multiply and combine them in strange ways to see what kinds of patterns emerge. Is 6 a prime number? Nope, because it has 1, 6, 2, and 3 as factors. Numbers that are not prime are called **composite numbers.** Is 5 a prime number? Yes, its only factors are 1 and 5. Is 2 a prime number? Yes, its only factors are 1 and itself. In fact, 2 is the only *even* prime number. Is 1 a prime number? Actually, this may surprise you. No, 1 is not a prime number. Why? Because 1 has so many unique characteristics that mathematicians think it belongs in a class all by itself. Mathematicians say that 1 is a **unit**, and they call that a special, separate category from primes and composites.

Now that you know how to multiply the smaller numbers in the times table, you will find that to multiply larger numbers is similar and quite simple. It just takes a little more time because there are more numbers involved. You multiply larger numbers one digits place at a time.

Let's start with 5×20. 5×0 equals 0, so write down 0. Now do 5×2. That equals 10. Write down 10 on the left of 0. That's the answer: 100.

You see, even though 5×0 is nothing, it's important to write down the 0 because it occupies the units place; that way when you multiply 5×2, you put the answer in the right place. If you had forgotten to put down the 0, you'd have gotten 5×20 equals 10, and that is definitely wrong. The only hard part in multiplying (once you know your times tables) is keeping the places straight.

Let's try 23 × 5. First multiply 5 × 3. That equals 15. Now multiply 5 × 2. Don't forget that the 2 is in the tens place, so it isn't really 2 at all, but 20. While 5 × 2 is 10, 5 times a 2 in the tens place is 5 × 20 or 100. Add 15 to 100. The answer is 115. (If you write out a string of 23 fives and add them all up, you should get 115. We don't recommend you do that, though, because it would be really dull.)

Can you multiply 5 × 123? That's 5 × 3 = 15, 5 × 20 = 100, and 5 × 100, which is 500. Now add 500 + 100 + 15. The answer is 615. These are illustrations of an important rule called the **distributive law**. When a mathematician writes it out in symbols, it looks like this: $a(b + c) = ab + ac$. In simple English, it says that when you want to multiply a number times a sum, you can multiply the number times each of the numbers in the sum and then add. In our last example, $5(100 + 20 + 3) = 5 \times 100 + 5 \times 20 + 5 \times 3 = 500 + 100 + 15 = 615$.

There's other way to do all this. Instead of breaking a number like 123 into 100, 20, and 3 to multiply by five in three very separate steps, we can compress the whole multiplication operation a little by carrying and do 5 × 123 all in one step. It's very much like the carrying we did in addition.

Let's try 5 × 123 again. We start, just as before, with 5 × 3. The answer is still 15, but this time we only write down the number on the right, 5 ones, and we carry the number on the left, 1 ten.

$$
\begin{array}{r}
{\scriptstyle 1} \\
123 \\
\times 5 \\
\hline
5
\end{array}
$$

Now we multiply just like before, 5×2. The answer is 10. Now add the number you carried; $10 + 1$ is 11. Just like before, write down the number on the right, 1, and carry the number on the left, 1.

$$\begin{array}{r} {\scriptstyle 1\ 1} \\ 123 \\ \times 5 \\ \hline 15 \end{array}$$

Now multiply 5×1, which equals 5, and add the number you carried, 1. $5 + 1$ is 6.

$$\begin{array}{r} {\scriptstyle 1\ 1} \\ 123 \\ \times 5 \\ \hline 615 \end{array}$$

Okay, one more: 23×15. First do $5 \times 3 = 15$. Write down the 5 and carry the 1. Now do $5 \times 2 = 10$, and don't forget to add the 1 that you carried.

$$\begin{array}{r} {\scriptstyle 1} \\ 23 \\ \times 15 \\ \hline 115 \end{array}$$

Now it's time to multiply by the 1 in 15. Because that 1 is in the tens place you're really multiplying by 10, but you know that multiplying by 10 is the same as multiplying by 1 and adding a 0. So you're going to put a 0 in the ones place, and then multiply by 1. That 0 will make sure that all the digits wind up in the correct columns.

$$\begin{array}{r} {\scriptstyle 1} \\ 23 \\ \times 15 \\ \hline 115 \\ +0 \\ \hline \end{array}$$

Now you just multiply 1×3 (which is 3) and 1×2 (which is 2) and write those down.

$$\begin{array}{r} {\scriptstyle 1} \\ 23 \\ \times 15 \\ \hline 115 \\ +230 \\ \hline \end{array}$$

Add it all up.

$$\begin{array}{r} {\scriptstyle 1} \\ 23 \\ \times 15 \\ \hline 115 \\ +230 \\ \hline 345 \\ \end{array}$$

Pay attention to how those digits are lined up, and you'll never have any trouble with multiplication.

MULTIPLICATION REVIEW

1. $4 \times 10 =$

2. $3 \times 14 =$

3. $14 \times 17 =$

4. $23 \times 14 =$

5. $517 \times 24 =$

6. Jennifer has 2 groups of 5 books each. How many books does she have?

7. Taylor has 10 jars of jellybeans, and each jar contains exactly 7 jellybeans. How many jellybeans does Taylor have in total?

8. Sondra has 10 boxes, and inside each box are 10 spiders. How many spiders does Sondra have in total?

9. Taylor has 22 separate cases, and inside each case are exactly 33. How many racecars does Taylor have? Before you even do the problem, do you think he has more than one thousand or fewer than 1,000?

10. Jennifer has been collecting decorative buttons for a long time. In her bedroom, she has exactly 103 jars, each filled with 43 buttons. How many buttons are in her collection? Before you do the problem, do you think she has more or fewer than 500 buttons? Does she have more or fewer than one thousand buttons?

DIVISION

Division helps you figure out how to break up numbers into smaller groups of equal size. Division isn't very complicated; it's just the opposite of multiplication. Remember a few pages back when you circled numbers of friends? We decided to look at that problem as a multiplication problem. We might very well have looked at it as a division problem and said, "Well, if I have 20 presents, how can I divide them evenly among 5 friends?" How would we answer this question? We have 20 presents, and we want to divide them into 5 groups, 1 group for each friend. You would make five groups of 4 presents each.

Everyone has an equal number of presents. From your multiplication table you know that $5 \times 4 = 20$, so $20 \div 5 = 4$. And there's another good reason to know your times table. Because division is the reverse of multiplication, we could just as easily call the times table the division table.

There are a few ways you will see the division operation written out in math. "Twenty divided by five" can look like any of these.

$$20 \div 5 \qquad 5\overline{)20} \qquad {}^{20}\!/_5$$

No matter how it looks, division is the opposite of multiplication. A number is always divisible by its factors. (Remember factors?) **Divisible** means the number can be evenly divided, with nothing left over. How does this work? Well, any number divided by 1 is itself. What is $20 \div 1$? It's 20. How about $9,999,999 \div 1$? That's 9,999,999. (By the way, how do you say that number? Nine million, nine hundred ninety-nine thousand, nine hundred ninety-nine. Whew!)

Okay, let's say you're dividing up those presents again, and this time you've decided to give presents to just 2 of your friends because the other 3 acted like jerks the last time you saw them. Now you've got 20 presents to divide between just two friends. Here's what the problem would look like: $2\overline{)20}$.

Usually, when you divide a two-digit number, you go 1 digit at a time, starting at the left. Does 2 go into 2? Yes, it goes in once. That's because any number divided by itself is equal to 1. So, you put a 1 on top, above the 2.

$$\begin{array}{r} 1 \\ 2\overline{)20} \end{array}$$

Now let's look at the next digit. How many groups of 2 are there in 0? There are none, so you write a 0 above this place. That's because 0 divided by any number is equal to 0.

$$\begin{array}{r} 10 \\ 2\overline{)20} \end{array}$$

Each friend would get ten presents. That means you can divide the presents down the middle into two equal halves. Any number that can be divided into 2 equal groups is called **even**. In other words, if you can divide a number by 2 without any left over, that number is even. If there is something left over when you divide the number by 2, that number is called **odd**.

Do you think 0 is even? Try it out. Two people want to share 0 cookies evenly. How many will each person get? 0. Will there be any left over? Nope, so 0 is divisible by 2; 0 is even. Can you divide 3 cookies evenly between 2 people? (And no breaking cookies, we're talking about whole cookies here.) No, there will always be one left over, so 3 is not even; 3 is odd.

Remember how you checked your subtraction by adding the answer and the smaller number to see if you got the bigger number? If you thought that $183 - 19 = 164$, you checked by adding $164 + 19$. If you got 183 (and you do), then your subtraction is correct. You can check your division by multiplying. If you have to divide $405 \div 5$, and you think the answer is 81, you can check by multiplying. If $81 \times 5 = 405$, your division is correct.

THINK ABOUT THIS

You can never divide any number by 0. Why? Well, suppose you tried to divide $54 \div 0$. First of all, trying to ask "how many groups of 0 are in 54?" is almost impossible to think about. Let's imagine, however, that you made a guess. Let's pretend you guessed there were 108 groups of 0 in 54. You would check by asking whether 108×0 was 54. It's not, of course. $108 \times 0 = 0$, not 54. If you changed your guess to 612 (to pick a number at random) and then checked, you'd find that 612×0 was still 0. No matter what you guessed, any number times 0 is 0. You can never get 54 by multiplying by 0. There is no correct answer to the problem $54 \div 0$.

To be fair, mathematicians don't exactly say, "You can't do it." They say, "Division by 0 is undefined." When mathematicians say something is undefined, it means one of two things: either there is no answer, or there are different possible answers. Either way, when it's undefined, it's off limits. We don't even try to do it. So we never divide by 0.

Okay, here's a question: You have 120 presents. Can you divide them evenly among five friends, and if you can, how many presents does each friend get? To answer the first part of this question, ask yourself whether 120 is divisible by 5. What do you think? Do you remember about the fives column? Look back to your times table. All of the numbers in the fives columns ended in 5 or 0. The truth is, any number ending in 5 or 0, no matter how big or how small, is divisible by 5. Is 120 divisible by 5? Yes, it's definitely divisible by 5.

Next, set up your division problem. You want to divide 120 into five groups, one for each kid, so 120 is what is being divided. It goes under the roof.

$$5\overline{)120}$$

Start with the left-most number. How many fives are there in 1? None, so you need to move to the right and try with a bigger number. (Technically, you could put a 0 over the 1, but we don't usually start a number with a 0.) Instead of just the left-most number, you combine it with the one next to it.

$$5\overline{)\underline{12}0}$$

How many 5s are there in 12? There are 2 fives in 12. Write 2 above the 12. You are probably saying to yourself, "But two fives makes 10, not 12. What do I do with the difference?" Well, you're on the right track. Two fives do make 10; to check your work and make the problem easier, you are going to write that 10 down below the 12.

$$
\begin{array}{r}
2 \\
5\overline{)120} \\
-10 \\
\hline
\end{array}
$$

Now subtract the 10 from the 12 to see how many you have left over.

$$
\begin{array}{r}
2 \\
5\overline{)120} \\
-\,10 \\
\hline
2
\end{array}
$$

You still have that 0 on the end. To finish off this division problem, drop that last digit down to join your leftover 2.

$$
\begin{array}{r}
2 \\
5\overline{)120} \\
-\,10 \\
\hline
20
\end{array}
$$

How many 5s are there in 20? There are four. Write that down above that last digit, and you are done.

$$
\begin{array}{r}
24 \\
5\overline{)120} \\
-\,10 \\
\hline
20 \\
-\,20 \\
\hline
0
\end{array}
$$

You can check your work now by multiplying what is on top by what is on the outside. That means multiply 24 by 5. Does it give you 120? It sure does. The great thing is that this will work on any division problem. Always check your work this way, and you can be sure to get more problems right.

ANOTHER THING TO THINK ABOUT

To check if an integer is divisible by 2 (or even, in other words), look at its units digit. If the units digit is even, then the whole number is even.

Sometimes (quite often, in fact) something you want to divide doesn't divide up evenly. Suppose you had 10 cookies to divide among 3 friends. Each friend would get 3 cookies. 3×3 is 9. There'd be 1 cookie left over. What if you counted yourself in the problem? Now there are 10 cookies to be divided among 4 people. Each person would get 2 cookies and there'd be 2 left over. This is called leaving a **remainder**. A remainder is what's left over when a number does not divide evenly.

Let's say you've got 19 cookies to divide among 5 friends.

$$5\overline{)19}$$

How many fives are in 1? None, so move to the next whole number. How many fives are in 19? There is room for three fives in 19. Subtract to find how many are left.

$$
\begin{array}{r}
3 \\
5\overline{)19} \\
-15 \\
\hline
4
\end{array}
$$

Hmmm, 5 isn't going to divide into 4 evenly, no matter what we do. So 4 is the remainder. This is usually written 3 r4.

For the extra special gold star, how about if you divide 4 by 5 anyway? How many groups of 5 are there in 4? None. And how many are left over? Well, the original 4 you tried to divide into never got divided, so that 4 is still left over. So, the answer is 0 r4. Later on, you'll learn to express the answer to a problem like this as a **fraction** or a **decimal**, but 0 r4 will do for now.

Are you ready for a tougher one? Let's take a couple of ugly numbers, the kind you just know aren't going to work out. Let's divide 714 by 17. It's a tough job, but somebody's got to do it. The truth is that this division problem will be a breeze if we just take it swtep by step.

First, how many groups of 17 will fit in 7? None; 7 is not big enough, so try 71. Can groups of 17 fit into 71? Sure they can. How many? Well, here is where your approximating skills will make life easier. 17 is approximately 20, and 71 is approximately 70. Twenty can fit into 70 about 3 times with a little more left over. The first number you are going to try on top is 3. Write it down and do the multiplication and subtraction.

$$
\begin{array}{r}
3 \\
17\overline{)714} \\
-51 \\
\hline
20
\end{array}
$$

Now look at the result of the subtraction, 20. It's bigger than 17, right? You can squeeze another group of 17 out of there, can't you? This means that 3 is too small. You need to try another number. Erase the 3 (that's why we use pencil) and try the next-biggest number, which is 4.

$$
\begin{array}{r}
4 \\
17\overline{)714} \\
-68 \\
\hline
3
\end{array}
$$

That's much better; now drop the 4 from the end of 714, and you have 34.

$$
\begin{array}{r}
4 \\
17\overline{)714} \\
-68\downarrow \\
\hline
34
\end{array}
$$

How many times does 17 go into 34? Exactly two. Put that up on top and multiply to check it.

$$
\begin{array}{r}
42 \\
17\overline{)714} \\
-68\downarrow \\
\hline
34 \\
-34 \\
\hline
0
\end{array}
$$

Perfect. 714 divided by 17 is exactly 42. By the way, that number 42, the answer to the problem, is called the **quotient**. A quotient is simply a fancy name for the result of a division problem.

Need a little help to remember the steps in division? Can you remember this silly sentence?

Do monkeys sleep completely bare?

The first letter of each work will remind you of a step in division.

Do	monkeys	sleep	completely	bare?
Divide	**Multiply**	**Subtract**	**Compare**	**Bring down**
Estimate how many times your divisor will go in. Put that number up top.	Multiply the number you just put up top times your divisor and write the answer underneath.	Subtract the product to see how much of a remainder you have.	Is the remainder smaller than the divisor? If not, erase and try a bigger number up top.	If there are more digits, bring one down and repeat the steps.

DIVISION REVIEW

1. $3\overline{)6}$

2. $3\overline{)24}$

3. $3\overline{)28}$

4. $6\overline{)132}$

5. $12\overline{)132}$

6. Sondra has 8 pictures she wants to hang on the 4 walls of her room, and she wants each wall to have the same number of pictures. How many pictures will each wall have?

7. Taylor has 32 bugs in his bug collection. He wants to arrange them on 8 velvet display boards, with each board having the same number of bugs. How many bugs will be on each board?

8. Jennifer has 3 friends over to tea, and she has made 35 sandwiches (she was feeling a trifle hungry). If she and her 3 friends each get the same number of sandwiches, how many will each of them get, and will any be left over? (And if any are left over, how many?)

9. Taylor has 225, but only 9 shirt drawers. If every drawer must have the same number of shirts (his parents are real sticklers for neatness), how many shirts will each drawer have?

10. Jennifer has agreed to visit the local children's hospital, and distribute her absolutely cool animal tooth collection. She has 252 teeth in the collection, including shark and bear teeth, and there are 16 sick kids in the hospital. If she promised to give each kid the same number of teeth, how many teeth will each kid get? And, just to approximate before you do the problem, will they get more or fewer than twenty each?

THINK ABOUT THIS

You can tell if a number is divisible by 3 by adding up that number's digits and seeing if they form a number divisible by three. If they do, the original number is evenly divisible by 3. For example, is 423 divisible by 3? Well, 4 + 2 + 3 = 9. Since 9 is evenly divisible by 3, we know that 423 is as well!

CHAPTER 12

Conquer Math Anxiety

Imagine this. You notice your heart beating. You don't usually notice that. Is it beating harder? Is it beating faster? Louder? Can other people hear it too? The little hairs on the back of your neck stand up, and your hands sweat so badly that you can't hold on to anything. You try to take a deep breath, but you feel like you can't get any air. Your mind is racing, and you can't concentrate. You want to run but you're afraid your legs won't hold you.

OK, stop imagining and take a deep breath. Hopefully, you'll never feel as terrible as that image, but if something like that were to happen to you during the latest horror movie or on some crazy thrill ride, well, that would be understandable. But during a math test? Absolutely unacceptable!

Years ago, people started to use the phrase "math anxiety" to refer to the nervousness and fear that some people feel when faced with math problems. Can it really be as horrible as that description? For some people, yes, but for most of the people who feel some math anxiety, it's a milder reaction. Of course, if it happens to you, that really doesn't matter much. It's unpleasant, and it means that you can't concentrate on the work you need to do.

Why do people react this way to math? Well, that's a complicated question that probably has a lot of answers, but one of the reasons is that people keep on believing an old myth about math: you either get it, or you don't. No one knows who started the rumor that some people are born with the ability to learn math and some people aren't, but it's a preposterous idea. Sure, we all have different talents, but that doesn't mean we can't learn the things we find more difficult. Could you imagine someone saying, "You either know how to read or you don't"? Would you believe someone who said "I'll never be able to learn history"?

Anyone can learn math. Not everyone will prove to be a mathematical genius, but anyone can do math by simply learning how to study the subject properly. The problem is that a lot of people don't know how to study math. Do you start to get a little nervous when you face a page full of fractions? Do decimals make you sweat? One way that you can avoid becoming a victim of math anxiety is to develop strong study skills, so here are a few tips that may help.

START AT THE BEGINNING

Don't wait until the day before the test to start studying. Start studying at the beginning of the year, the beginning of the book, or even the beginning of each chapter. Begin to study and to prepare for tests as soon as your teacher introduces new material.

READ THE BOOK

Yes, you can read a math book. You just read this one, didn't you? Read the explanations several times. Take your time and really focus on what is being said. Try to restate what you've read in your own words. Take notes as you read. Make a list of questions to ask in class.

The examples are not just there to prove the author knows how to do the math, they're meant to be models for you to follow. Try covering the solution and doing the problem on your own. After each step, uncover a line and see if your solution matches the one in the book.

Most people don't look at the textbook until they sit down to do homework, but if you read the section of the book that you expect your teacher to cover tomorrow, the explanations given in class will be easier to follow, and you'll already have an idea about what questions you want to ask.

Sometimes they're blue, or red, or green, or pink, but just about every math book has boxes that discuss important information. You can be fairly sure that this material will be part of the notes your teacher wants you to take. For many students, getting that information copied from the board into their notebooks is a slow, difficult process, especially when there are lots of details or special symbols. While they're trying to get the information from the chalkboard into their notes, they may miss something else important.

If you copy the material in the boxes into your notebook ahead of time, you can really listen to the teacher's explanation without having to copy frantically. If you're not sure where in your notes to put the information, you might copy it onto an index card ahead of time, and just tape the card into your notebook at the right spot. It might even be enough just to write "See blue box at the top of page 43."

Yes, there are a lot of special words and symbols that you need to learn for math class, but there are a lot of special words and symbols you need to learn for your other classes too. Is it easier to say "deux plus trois égales cinq," "dos más tres iguales cinco" or "二加上三均等五" than to say "2 + 3 = 5"? Is it really harder to learn to read $4 + 5(3 - x) + 2\left[3 - 2(x + 5)\right]$ than it is to read this:

Have a pencil, a notebook, a ruler, and a calculator (if your teacher allows them). If you're learning to graph, have graph paper. If you're learning to measure angles, have a protractor. You wouldn't show up for a softball game without a bat, ball, or glove, would you?

Homework is your chance to find out if you really understand what was covered in class, to practice the new skills, and to make your mistakes and learn from them. Don't skip it because you think the problems are easy, and don't give up if you find out it's difficult.

And write it down. With a problem like $3 + 5(18 - 7 \cdot 2) - 12$, if you write down nothing but 11, it won't matter that you got the right answer. In a few weeks or a few months, when it's time to study for a test or an exam, will you know how you got it? If you write down the entire problem, it's much easier to see what was done.

Mistakes are an important step in learning, but only if you stop to understand what you did wrong and why. It's nice to know what the correct answer is, but unless you take the time to understand your mistakes, you'll keep making them. Re-work problems you got wrong, and be certain you understand how to do them.

If you play an instrument, you know that your first attempt at a song sounded terrible. Only lots of practice got you to a point where your music was pleasant. Learning math takes time to think about things and practice to build skills. Be patient with yourself.

So you've prepared, and you've practiced, and you've done a good job of studying, and it's time for the test. How do you ward off feelings of panic? The most important tip sounds so obvious it seems silly: study. Don't fall into that trap of thinking you just have to "get it." Review your notes, read your textbook, rework some problems from your homework. Don't leave all your studying until the night before the test. Start doing a little each day as soon as you know the date of the test. That will give you time to ask your teacher any questions that come up. And don't study too much. After a while, going over and over the same material, all you do is make yourself nervous and tired.

That leads to another tip: Get a good night's sleep the night before the test. An extra hour of studying won't do any good if you're too tired to concentrate. You need to be well rested to do your best work. The morning of the test, eat a good breakfast. You want your mind to be on the problem you're solving, not on the growling in your stomach.

Suppose you've done all the right things up to the moment of the test, and then the test paper hits your desk and suddenly… blank. You can't remember anything. The test might as well be written in a foreign language. What do you do? First, take a deep breath. Close your eyes and remind yourself of all the work you've done to prepare. Open your eyes and write something down. Anything. Put your name on the paper. On a blank sheet, or the back of the test, or in the margins, write down anything you do remember from your studying. Don't worry about the questions yet, just write something. See, you do remember.

Now read the whole test. Don't stop reading after the first question. Read all the way through, and get the big picture of the test. You'll start to see things you remember how to do, and one question may give you a hint on how to do another. Do you hear a voice in your head telling you that you can't do this? Point to a question you do know how to do and tell the voice to be quiet.

Answer the questions you feel confident about first. This assures you those points and gets you into a working rhythm. As you finish more questions, your confidence will grow. When you face the questions that are more difficult, think about what you've done so far. What did you learn just after that, or just before? If you've studied all along, you should have a view of the material as a whole. Each question is a piece of that whole.

Don't stay with something that's going nowhere. If you're not making any progress on a question, move on to another one. You can come back later, if you have time, but you don't want to have time run out before you've done everything you know how to do.

Let's suppose you've done everything you're sure of and time is running out. What now? Go for the points you can get. Do you know how to do the second part of a question, but not the first? Say so. Write a note to your teacher. "I don't know how to do part A, but I'm going to make up an answer for it, so I can go on and show I know how to do part B." Then do just that: Make up an answer that seems reasonable for the first part and use it to finish the problem. You won't get full credit, but you may get some points, and you'll have shown your teacher that you're thinking about the process, not just the answer. If there is too little time to do even that much, write a quick summary of what you would do if there was enough time. "Square both sides, add the squares, and take square root."

Turn in that test paper, take another deep breath, and remember how much you did know. The test is over, and you can't change it now, so relax, forget about it, and move on to the new material. Remember that learning takes time and that we learn from mistakes too. When the test is returned, correct what you got wrong and celebrate what you got right. Think about what you learned from taking this test that might help you do better on the next one.

If you've read this far, it means that you're thinking about math and about how you learn math. That's a positive sign. If you let yourself believe that math is a list of formulas and rules to memorize, you could drown under all the memorizing you need to do, and you won't have a system for organizing all that information and retrieving it when you need it. If you're thinking about math, about the why and the how of math, you'll see why the rules make sense and how to use the formulas, and all the pieces will fit together.

Believe in yourself as a thinker. Believe in your ability to do math. Work hard and have fun with it. Celebrate your success.

FORMULA CHEAT SHEET

IMPORTANT FACTS AND FORMULAS

Order of Operations

PEMDAS or **P**lease **E**xcuse **M**y **D**ear **A**unt **S**ally remind us to do:

Parentheses, **E**xponents, **M**ultiplication and **D**ivision, **A**ddition and **S**ubtraction

Bowtie Method for Adding and Subtracting Fractions

$$\frac{a}{b} + \frac{c}{d} = \frac{a \times d + c \times b}{b \times d}$$

Percent Problems

$$\frac{part}{whole} = \frac{\%}{100}$$

Percent Change

$$\frac{change}{original} = \frac{\%}{100}$$

Probability

Probability of an event $= \dfrac{\text{number of ways it can happen}}{\text{number of all things that can happen}}$

Angles

Acute angles measure less than 90°

Right angles measure exactly 90°

Obtuse angles measure more than 90° and less than 180°

Straight angles measure exactly 90°

Triangles

Acute triangles have three acute angles

Right triangles have one right angle (and two acute angles)

Obtuse triangles have one obtuse angle (and two acute angles)

Equiangular triangles have three equal angles, each 60°

Equilateral triangles have three equal sides.
All equilateral triangles are equiangular

Isosceles triangles have two equal sides
Isosceles triangles have two equal angles, opposite the equal sides.

Scalene triangles have no equal sides. All three sides are of different lengths.

The **three angles of a triangle** always add to 180°
The **four angles of a quadrilateral** always add to 360°

Perimeter and Circumference

Perimeter of a polygon is the sum of the lengths of the sides

Perimeter of a rectangle = $2l + 2w$

Perimeter of a square = $4s$

Circumference of a circle $= \pi d = 2\pi r$, where d is the diameter and r is the radius

Area

Parallelogram	$A = bh$
Rectangle	$A = bh = lw$
Square	$A = s^2$
Triangle	$A = \dfrac{1}{2}bh$
Trapezoid	$A = \dfrac{1}{2}\left(b_1 + b_2\right)h$

Pythagorean Theorem

In any right triangle with legs a and b and hypotenuse c, $a^2 + b^2 = c^2$

Volume

Prism $\quad V = Bh$, where B is the area of the base and h is the height

Pyramid $\quad V = \dfrac{1}{3}Bh$, where B is the area of the base and h is the height

Cylinder $\quad V = \pi r^2 h$, where r is the radius of the base and h is the height

Cone $\quad V = \dfrac{1}{3}\pi r^2 h$, where r is the radius of the base and h is the height

GLOSSARY

GLOSSARY

Acute: An angle measuring less than 90 degrees.

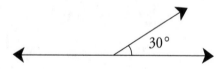

Add: To combine numbers or objects.

Angle: The shape created by two lines, segments or rays that have a common endpoint.

Approximation: Intelligent guessing about a size or amount.

Area: The surface covered by a shape.

Associative law of addition: A law that says the numbers in an addition problem will always add up to the same amount, no matter how they are grouped.

Average or arithmetic mean: A single number that gives a sense of the center of a group of numbers. The average is found by adding all the numbers and then dividing by the count.

Axes: The horizontal and vertical lines on which the measurements of a graph are marked. The horizontal line is called the *x*-axis and the vertical line is called *y*-axis.

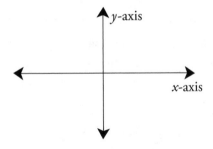

Base: The side of a shape that meets the height. It is usually the bottom.

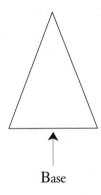

Base

Bimodal: A sample that contains two modes, or two numbers that both occur more frequently than the other numbers in the sample.

Borrowing: The process of take one from the next larger place digit and regrouping it as ten of the current place digits, to make subtraction possible.

$$\begin{array}{r} {}^{0}\cancel{1}\ {}^{1}5 \\ -\ \ \ 9 \\ \hline 6 \end{array}$$

Bow tie: A method of adding or subtracting fractions.

Cancellation: The process of finding common factors in the numerators and denominators of two fractions being multiplied, and dividing the numerator and denominator of the different fractions by this factor to make multiplication easier.

$$\frac{4}{3} \times \frac{9}{2} = \frac{36}{6} = \frac{6}{1} \qquad \frac{\overset{2}{\cancel{4}}}{\underset{1}{\cancel{3}}} \times \frac{\overset{3}{\cancel{9}}}{\underset{1}{\cancel{2}}} = \frac{6}{1}$$

Carrying: When the total of a column in an addition problem is more than one digit, the lowest place value digit is placed below the column, and the higher place digit is added over to the next column.

$$
\begin{array}{cc}
\overset{1}{} & \\
1 & 5 \\
+ & 9 \\
\hline
2 & 4 \\
\end{array}
$$

Cent: A root of many words in English. It means 100.

Circle: A closed, two-dimensional shape that is perfectly round, made up of all the points at a certain distance from a center.

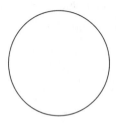

Circle graph: A graph showing a whole divided into parts with a circle cut into percentages.

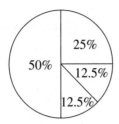

Circumference: The distance around a circle.

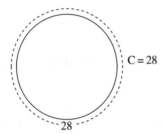

Coefficient: The number in front of a variable, by which the variable is multiplied. In 4x, for example, 4 is the coefficient of x, and the expression means 4 times x.

Combinations: Possible ways to choose various objects or people, without regard to the order in which they are to be arranged.

Common denominator: A multiple of all fraction denominators in a particular addition or subtraction problem.

Commutative law of addition: A law that says when you add numbers, the result is the same no matter what order those numbers are in.

Commutative law of multiplication: A law that says the result of multiplication will be the same no matter what order the numbers are in.

Cone: A closed, three-dimensional shape starting with a circle and narrowing to a point.

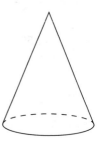

Congruent: Exactly equal in size and shape. Congruent shapes have the same measurements.

Cross-multiplying: Multiplying diagonally across an equal sign, usually to find a missing value.

Cube: A closed, three-dimensional shape with 6 squares for sides and 12 equal edges, and every angle a right angle (a square box).

Cubic units: Units in the shape of cubes used to measure the volume of three-dimensional figures.

Cylinder: A three-dimensional, closed tube, with equal-sized circles at either end.

Decimal: A fraction written as a number to the right of the decimal point, with a denominator that is a power of 10.

Decimal point: A dot placed to the direct right of the units digit in a number, to separate the whole from the fractional part. If there is no fractional part, the decimal point may not be shown.

$$459.1234$$
$$\uparrow$$
Decimal Point

Denominator: The bottom part of a fraction.

$$\frac{1}{2} \leftarrow \text{Denominator}$$

Diagonal: A line segment that passes from one vertex of a shape to another, through the interior of the shape.

$$\frac{1}{2} \leftarrow \text{Denominator}$$

Diameter: A line segment drawn through the center of a circle from 1 side to the other.

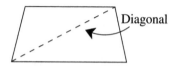

Diamond: A closed, four-sided, two-dimensional shape with 2 sets of equal angles.

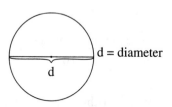

d = diameter

Digit: A number between 0 and 9.

Digit places: The spaces in a number occupied by digits. Each place gives the digit a different value: ones, tens, hundreds.

Dimensions: The measurement of a geometric shape: length, width, height.

Distributive law: A law that says multiplying a number times the sum of two numbers is the same as multiplying it by the first number and by the second and then adding the answers. Also known as: $a(b + c) = ab + ac$.

Divisible: A number is divisible by another if it can be divided into equal parts by the other number with no remainder.

Division: A way of separating a number into equal groups.

Equal angles: an obtuse pair of angles opposite one another, and an acute pair opposite one another.

Equation: A complete mathematical sentence containing an equal sign. The equal sign means that the expressions on either side of the sign are equivalent; that is, they ultimately represent the same number.

Equilateral triangle: A triangle with three equal sides and three equal angles.

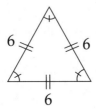

Even: A number that can be divided by 2 with no remainder.

Exponent: A small number placed at the upper right of another that tells you to multiply the base number times itself a certain number of times.

$$2^{3} \leftarrow \text{Exponent}$$

Extremes: The outside numbers in a proportion.

$$3 : 2 :: 6 : 4$$
Extremes

Factors: Numbers that multiply together to produce a certain product; for instance, 2 and 3 are factors of 6.

Fraction: A number expressed as part over whole, with a fraction bar.

Height: The length of a line drawn from the top of a shape to form a right angle with the base.

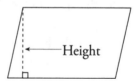

Hexagon: A closed, two-dimensional, six-sided shape.

Hundreds digit: The digit third from the right in a whole number and three to the left of the decimal point in a decimal.

Hundredths place: The digits place 2 to the right of the decimal point.

$$459.1234$$
↑
Hundredths Place

Hypotenuse: The side opposite the right angle in a right triangle.

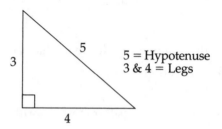

Improper fraction: A fraction in which the numerator is larger than the denominator. An improper fraction is worth more than one.

Independent events: Events whose outcomes have no effect on each other.

Infinity: Going on without end.

Intersection: The point where two lines cross.

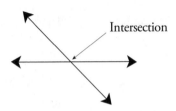

Intersection

Isolating the variable: Manipulating a mathematical expression so that the variable is alone on one side of the equal sign.

Isosceles triangle: A triangle with two equal sides and two equal angles opposite those sides.

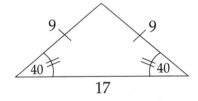

Legs: The shorter sides of a right triangle.

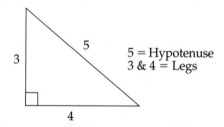

5 = Hypotenuse
3 & 4 = Legs

Length: The longer dimension of a quadrilateral.

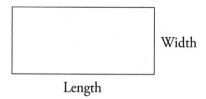

Width

Length

Line: A straight line that goes on forever, connecting at least two points.

Line graph: A graph made of a horizontal and a vertical axis, expressing the relationship between two sets of numbers.

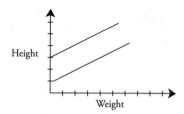

Height

Weight

Line segment: A section of a line between two endpoints.

Means: The inside numbers expressed in a proportion.

$$3:2::6:4$$
Means

Median: The middle number of a group of numbers.

Mixed number: A number that combines a fraction and a whole number, such as $6\frac{2}{5}$.

Mode: The most frequently occurring number in a group of numbers.

Multiple: The product of a number and another whole number; for instance, 12 is a multiple of 6.

Multiply: A quick way of adding a number to itself a certain number of times. Can be written as 2×3, $(2)(3)$, $2 \cdot 3$, or $2(3)$.

Negative number: A number less than 0.

Numerator: The top part of a fraction.

$$\frac{1}{2} \leftarrow \text{Numerator}$$

Obtuse: An angle measuring more than 90°.

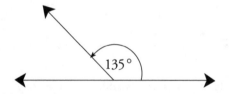

Octagon: A closed, two-dimensional, eight-sided shape.

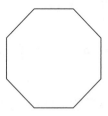

Odd: A number that cannot be evenly divided by 2.

Order of operations: The specific order—parentheses, exponents, multiplication and division, addition and subtraction—in which to do arithmetic problems.

Parallel: Lines that run together but remain an equal distance apart, never intersecting.

Parallelogram: A quadrilateral with two pairs of parallel sides.

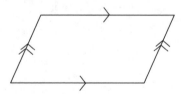

Parentheses or ( ): Punctuation marks surrounding parts of a math problem that indicate the part of the problem to be done first.

PEMDAS: (Please Excuse My Dear Aunt Sally) An acronym for the specific order in which to do arithmetic problems: parentheses, exponents, multiplication and division, addition and subtraction.

Pentagon: A closed, two-dimensional, five-sided shape.

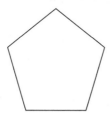

Percent or %: A way of expressing the amount per 100.

Perimeter: The length of the outside border of a closed shape.

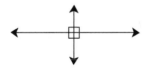

$$P = 6 + 13 + 6 + 13 = 38$$

Permutations: Possible arrangements of a group of objects or people.

Perpendicular: Two lines that meet to form right angles.

Pi or π: The ratio of the circumference of any circle to its diameter.

Pictograph: A graph showing information with little pictures.

Planar: Flat, two-dimensional.

Point: A mark that takes up no space.

Positive number: A number greater than 0.

Power: A number with an exponent.

Prime number: A number that has no factors other than itself and 1. Examples of prime numbers include 2, 3, 5, 7, 11, 13, 17, and 19. The number 1 is not prime.

Probability: The likelihood that something will happen, expressed as a fraction (or decimal or percent). The numerator of the fraction is the number of ways it can happen, and the denominator is the count of all the things that could possibly happen.

Product: The result of multiplication.

Proportion: Two equal ratios.

Protractor: An instrument used to measure the number of degrees in an angle.

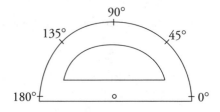

Pythagorean theorem: A law that says in a right triangle, the sum of the squares of the two legs is equal to the square of the hypotenuse; also known as: a2 + b2 = c2, where c is the hypotenuse.

Quadrilateral: A closed, two-dimensional, four-sided shape.

Quotient: The result of a division problem.

Radius: A length drawn from the center of a circle to the edge.

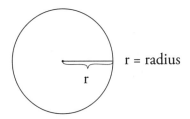

r = radius

Ratio: An expression showing the relative parts of a whole. A ratio of 2 to 3 can be shown as 2 : 3, or 2 to 3, or $\frac{2}{3}$.

Ratio box: A box used to help figure out answers to ratio questions.

Ray: A portion of a line beginning at a fixed point that then goes on forever.

Reciprocal: The inverse of a number. The reciprocal of 5 is $\frac{1}{5}$.

Rectangle: A closed, four-sided, two-dimensional shape with four right angles.

Reducing: The method of putting a fraction in its simplest form.

Remainder: What is left over when a number does not divide evenly.

Rhombus: A parallelogram with four equal sides.

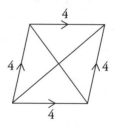

Right angle: An angle of exactly 90 degrees.

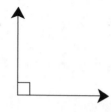

Right triangle: A triangle containing a right angle.

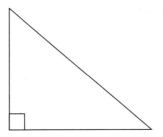

Round: To rewrite a number with fewer non-zero digits, by deciding whether it is closer to a number above it or a number below it with the desired number of digits.

Scale: An expression of the ratio of information to the lines on a graph, given in the graph.

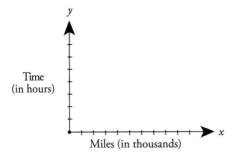

Side: The edge of a closed, two-dimensional shape.

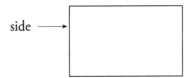

Similar: Two shapes of different sizes whose angles are the same and whose sides have the exact same ratio.

Sphere: A perfectly round, closed, three-dimensional globe.

Square: To multiply a number by itself.

Squares: Closed, four-sided, two-dimensional shapes with four right angles and equal sides.

Square units: Units in the shape of squares used to measure the area of two-dimensional figures.

Subtract: To take a number away from another.

Sum: The result of addition.

Tens digit: The digit second from the right on a whole number, and two to the left of the decimal point in a decimal.

$$459.1234$$
$$\uparrow$$
Tens Digit

Tenths place: The digits place directly to the right of the decimal point.

$$459.1234$$
$$\uparrow$$
Tenths Place

Thousandths place: The digits place three to the right of the decimal point.

$$459.1234$$
$$\uparrow$$
Thousandths Place

Three-dimensional: Taking up space or volume; not flat.

Times: Another way of saying, "multiplied by."

Trapezoid: A quadrilateral with two parallel sides and two non-parallel sides.

9.1234
↑
Tenths place

Triangles: Closed, three-sided, two-dimensional shapes.

9.1234
↑
Thousandths place

Two-dimensional: Flat.

Units digit: The digit furthest to the right in a whole number, and the first digit to the left of the decimal point in a decimal.

459.1234
↑
Units Digit

Variable: A letter that represents a number in an algebraic equation.

Vertex: The point or corner of an angle.

267.36
↑
Units digit

Vertices: The plural of vertex; points or corners of a shape or group of angles.

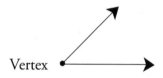

Vertex

Volume: The amount of space taken up by a three-dimensional shape.

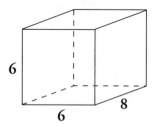

Width: The shorter dimension of a quadrilateral.

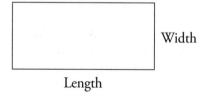

Width

Length

x-axis: The horizontal axis of a graph.

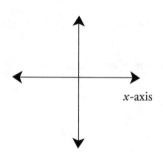

x-axis

y-axis: The vertical axis of a graph. y-axis.

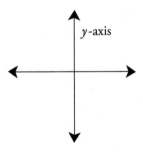

ANSWERS AND EXPLANATIONS

ARITHMETIC CHECK

1. 29, an odd number

   Since this problem has addition and subtraction only, you do it in the order it appears, left to right. So $17 + 34 = 51$, and $51 - 22 = 29$. Can you divide 29 evenly into two groups? Nope, so 29 is odd.

2. 205, an odd number and *not* a multiple of 3

   This is a little tricky unless you remember the order of operations. Multiplication and division come before addition and subtraction, so the first thing to do is the multiplication: $100 \times 3 = 300$. Then do the subtraction: $505 - 300 = 205$. Is 205 divisible into 2 equal groups? No, so it is odd. To find out whether 205 is divisible by 3, simply add up the digits, $2+0+5=7$. Is 7 divisible by 3? No, so the number 205 is not divisible by 3.

3. 104, which is even and is not a multiple of 5. It is also not prime.

   This one is longer, but just hold on and follow the order of operations. First, multiplication and division left to right, so $20 \times 3 = 60$, then $60 \div 4 = 15$. Then addition and subtraction left to right, $15 + 23 - 17 + 83 = 104$. Since 104 ends in an even number, it is even, and since it does not end in 5 or 0, it is not divisible by 5. How do you know whether it is prime? Well, it is divisible by 2, isn't it, because it's even? So that means 2 is one of its factors, and a prime number can only have 2 factors, itself and 1, so 104 is not prime.

4. 181, which is not a multiple of 5. And 181 divided by 3 is 60 r1.

   Are you getting the hang of these yet? The division and multiplication always comes first and goes left to right, so $234 \div 6 = 39$, and $39 \times 2 = 78$. Then the addition, $78+103=181$. Does 181 end in 5 or 0? No, so it is not a multiple of 5. Divide 181 by 3 and you get 60 r1.

5. 725, which is a multiple of 5, but it is neither a multiple of 3 nor a prime number.

   You perform multiplication and division first, right? So, $309 \times 25 = 7,725$. Then, $7,725 \div 15 = 515$, then you have $200+515+10=725$. This is a multiple of 5 because it ends in 5, but $7+2+5=14$, and 14 is not divisible by 3, so 725 is not divisible by 3. Is it a prime number? Well, you know it is divisible by 5, so 5 is a factor of 725. That means that 725 has more factors than just itself and 1, so it is *not* prime.

6. 8 autographed baseballs

   Because $37 - 29 = 8$. That's all there is to this problem!

7. 81 strawberries. (Estimate about 75 strawberries.)

   To estimate, round 27 down to 25 and $25 \times 3 = 75$. Each basket has 27 berries, and 3 times that means the problem should read 25×3, which equals 81.

8. 2 ice cream sandwiches each, with 2 left over

   Sondra and her 11 friends make up a total of 12 people sharing in this pool of 26 ice cream sandwiches. So, $26 \div 12$ is 2, with a remainder of 2. That can also be expressed as 2 r2.

9. 6,526 pounds of books

That's a lot of books! This is a multiplication problem; he does a load of 251 twenty-six times, so $251 \times 26 = 6,526$.

10. 36 maps, with $6 left over

This is a little bit more complicated, but it uses the same operations you've been using the whole time. First, how much money does Jennifer have? Each of 14 relatives gave her $39, so $14 \times 39 = \$546$. Now she needs to know how many groups of $15 she can get out of the $546. So she divides the 546 into groups of 15: $546 \div 15$. 15 goes into 546 36 times, with 6 left over at the bottom. So she could buy 36 maps and still have $6 left for something else.

QUIZ # 2

FRACTIONS

1. $\dfrac{2}{5}$

There are a total of 5 pieces in the whole and 2 of them are shaded, so 2 is the part over the whole of 5.

2. $\dfrac{1}{5}$

There are 10 parts to the whole, and 2 of them are shaded, so the fraction is $\dfrac{2}{10}$. To reduce this fraction, divide both the top and the bottom by 2. $\dfrac{2 \div 2}{10 \div 2} = \dfrac{1}{5}$

3. $\dfrac{3}{4}+\dfrac{1}{5}=\dfrac{19}{20}$

Whew! The pie in the picture has 12 of 16 parts shaded. $\dfrac{12}{16}$ can be reduced, first by 2 to $\dfrac{6}{8}$ and then by 2 again to $\dfrac{3}{4}$, or you could have reduced all at once by 4. The fraction of the pie in question 2 was $\dfrac{1}{5}$. To figure out $\dfrac{3}{4}+\dfrac{1}{5}$ you can use bow tie, and the answer is $\dfrac{19}{20}$. The answer cannot be reduced, so it's already in its simplest form.

4. $\dfrac{21}{10}=2\dfrac{1}{10}$

To subtract mixed numbers, convert them to improper fractions first. So $3\dfrac{1}{2}$ becomes $\dfrac{7}{2}$ and $1\dfrac{2}{5}$ becomes $\dfrac{7}{5}$, and the question looks like this: $\dfrac{7}{2}-\dfrac{7}{5}$ Then you can use the bow tie to get $\dfrac{35-14}{2\times5}$. That will eventually give you $\dfrac{21}{10}$, which can reduce to $2\dfrac{1}{10}$.

5. $\dfrac{67}{6}$ or $11\dfrac{1}{6}$

To add mixed numbers, convert them to improper fractions. So $9\dfrac{2}{3}$ becomes $\dfrac{29}{3}$ and $1\dfrac{1}{2}$ becomes $\dfrac{3}{2}$. $\dfrac{29}{3}+\dfrac{3}{2}=\dfrac{67}{6}$ Then convert to a mixed number: 6 goes into 67 eleven times, with 1 left over.

6. $\frac{3}{4}$

Draw a picture to see how this works. Divide the pie into 4 so there are quarters, and then shade in the quarter of Rose's and the 2 other quarters that belong to her friends. That is 3 parts of the pie out of a possible 4, so $\frac{3}{4}$.

7. $\frac{4}{4}$, better known as 1 whole bag of candy

He starts out with $\frac{1}{4}$ and then adds $\frac{1}{2}$ and another $\frac{1}{4}$. Use a common denominator of 4, then add the numerators. $\frac{1}{4}+\frac{1}{2}+\frac{1}{4}=\frac{1}{4}+\frac{2}{4}+\frac{1}{4}=\frac{4}{4}$ and $\frac{4}{4}$, just like any number over itself, is equal to 1. $8\frac{1}{2}$

8. $\frac{18}{35}$; more than $\frac{1}{2}$

Sondra had $\frac{6}{7}$, and her sister took $\frac{2}{5}$ of Sondra's portion of the cake. $\frac{2}{5}\times\frac{6}{7}=\frac{12}{35}$. Sondra's sister took $\frac{12}{35}$ of the cake. Now you need to subtract $\frac{12}{35}$ from $\frac{6}{7}$. Can you see an easy common denominator? Sure, 35 is a multiple of 7, so $\frac{6}{7}-\frac{12}{35}=\frac{30}{35}-\frac{12}{35}=\frac{18}{35}$. $\frac{18}{35}$ is more than half, but just barely. How can you tell? Well, one way is to look at the numerator (18). Is it half of the denominator (35)?

It's a little more.

9. $\dfrac{51}{6}$ or $\dfrac{17}{2}$ or checker sets

To add mixed numbers, convert them to improper fractions! $3\dfrac{2}{3}+4\dfrac{5}{6}$ becomes $\dfrac{11}{3}+\dfrac{29}{6}$. You can use the bow tie method, or ask yourself if one denominator is a multiple of another. Yes, 6 is multiple of 3, so you can just transform $\dfrac{11}{3}$ by multiplying it by $\dfrac{2}{2}$ to become $\dfrac{22}{6}$. Then, $3\dfrac{2}{3}+4\dfrac{5}{6}=\dfrac{11}{3}+\dfrac{29}{6}=\dfrac{22}{6}+\dfrac{29}{6}=\dfrac{51}{6}$. Reduce the fraction by dividing by 3, or make into a mixed number.

10. $\dfrac{55}{8}$ or $6\dfrac{7}{8}$

Transform to a fraction, then subtract: $10\dfrac{3}{4}$ becomes $\dfrac{43}{4}$, and $3\dfrac{7}{8}$ becomes $\dfrac{31}{8}$. Can you see an easy common denominator? Sure, 8 is a multiple of 4, so $\dfrac{43}{4}$ becomes $\dfrac{86}{8}$. Then $\dfrac{86}{8}-\dfrac{31}{8}=\dfrac{55}{8}$. And yes, she did have enough fake blood after the spill. You could estimate that she would have more than six gallons left after the spill. How? Well, she had *more* than 10 gallons at the start, and she lost *less* than 4 gallons in the spill. She must have *more* than 6 gallons left.

MULTIPLYING AND DIVIDING FRACTIONS

1. $\dfrac{1}{6}$

   To multiply fractions, just multiply the tops and the bottoms straight across.

2. $\dfrac{2}{45}$

3. 1

   Did you realize that this could be written $\dfrac{\frac{1}{2}}{\frac{1}{2}}$? Any number over itself is equal to 1.

4. $\dfrac{7}{3}$

   Just convert the mixed numbers to fractions. Then you can cancel.

   $$\frac{7}{\cancel{2}_{1}} \times \frac{\cancel{2}^{1}}{3} = \frac{7}{3}$$

5. $\dfrac{30}{47}$

   Once you convert these to improper fractions and flip them over, you can cancel and multiply. $3\dfrac{1}{3} \div 5\dfrac{2}{9} = \dfrac{10}{3} \div \dfrac{47}{9} = \dfrac{10}{3} \times \dfrac{9}{47}$ The 9 and the 3 cancel, so you'll be left with $\dfrac{10}{\cancel{3}_{1}} \times \dfrac{\cancel{9}^{3}}{47} = \dfrac{30}{47}$

6. $4\dfrac{4}{5}$

To make this easier, first you need to figure out what the problem is asking. The $\dfrac{1}{3}$ question is asking how many bags he will give away. Well, in a way, the answer is right there: It says he will give away $\dfrac{4}{5}$ of the marbles he has, or $\dfrac{4}{5}$ of 6. You know that when you see the word "of," it means multiply so $\dfrac{4}{5} \times 6 = \dfrac{24}{5}$. Remember, 6 can just be written as $\dfrac{6}{1}$ to make the problem easier to look at. And of course, the answer will be less than 6 because the question is asking for a fractional part of 6.

7. 28

This question asks how many slices exist within the pizza she has, so it is really asking you to divide the pizza she has into slices. "Divide" is the operative word here. So the $\dfrac{7}{8}$ pizza is being divided into slices, $\dfrac{1}{32} \cdot \dfrac{7}{8} \div \dfrac{1}{32}$ becomes $\dfrac{7}{8} \times \dfrac{32}{1}$. Can you cancel now that you have flipped it? Certainly.

$$\dfrac{7}{\cancel{8}_1} \times \dfrac{\cancel{32}^{4}}{1} = \dfrac{7}{1} \times \dfrac{4}{1} = \dfrac{28}{1} = 28$$

8. $\dfrac{1}{15}$

What word in this problem tips you off that it is a multiplication problem? The word "of," as in "he wants to give his brother *of* it." So $\dfrac{1}{5} \times \dfrac{1}{3} = \dfrac{1}{15}$.

9. $\dfrac{7}{10}$

Again, you see the word "of" in "She wants to take $\dfrac{1}{5}$ *of* their cantaloupe stash," so you know you are dealing with a multiplication problem. So convert that mixed number to a fraction, and you have $\dfrac{7}{2} \times \dfrac{1}{5} = \dfrac{7}{10}$. This is less than 1, and you could have approximated to yourself, "Well, one-fifth, hmmm, if they had 5 that means she would take 1. Since they have less than 5, she will take less than 1."

10. $\dfrac{112}{5}$ or $22\dfrac{2}{5}$

You probably knew this was a division problem by the way the question asked, "How many $\dfrac{1}{4}$ bags of bugs does she have in her collection?" So convert $5\dfrac{3}{5}$ to a fraction, $\dfrac{28}{5}$, and divide by $\dfrac{1}{4}$. As long as you didn't make the deadly mistake of canceling before you flipped over the second fraction, you should have ended with $\dfrac{28}{5} \times \dfrac{4}{1} = \dfrac{112}{5}$.

REVIEW

1. $\dfrac{3}{6}$ and $\dfrac{1}{2}$ are equal. The others reduce to $\dfrac{1}{5}$, $\dfrac{2}{3}$, and $\dfrac{2}{5}$.

2. $\dfrac{5}{6}$

   Use the bow tie!

3. $\dfrac{9}{8}$ or $1\dfrac{1}{8}$

   Just invert the second fraction and multiply. *Never cancel in a division problem before you invert the fraction and change the operation to multiply!*

4. $\dfrac{11}{8}$ or $1\dfrac{3}{8}$

   Convert $3\dfrac{2}{3}$ to a fraction and multiply straight across. It becomes $\dfrac{3}{8} \times \dfrac{11}{3}$, and you can cancel because the question is in multiplication form. $\dfrac{\cancel{3}^{1}}{8} \times \dfrac{11}{\cancel{3}_{1}} = \dfrac{11}{8}$

5. $\dfrac{7}{11}$

   Convert to fractions, invert the second one, and multiply. You get $\dfrac{7}{2} \times \dfrac{2}{11}$, and the 2s cancel.

6. No.

Does $\frac{2}{3}$ equal $\frac{3}{6}$? Well, see if the fractions are in their most reduced forms. Do 2 and 3 have any common multiples? Nope, so $\frac{2}{3}$ is in its most reduced form. Do 3 and 6 have any common multiples? Yes, they are both divisible by 3, so you can reduce $\frac{3}{6}$. It becomes $\frac{1}{2}$. Does $\frac{2}{3} = \frac{1}{2}$? Nope. You can also draw a picture to help you see why. Divide a circle into 3 parts and shade in 2 of them for the $\frac{2}{3}$. Then draw a circle the same size, divide it into 2 parts, and shade in 1 of them for the $\frac{1}{2}$. Is the same amount shaded both times? No way, so the fractions are not equal.

7. $\frac{1}{6}$

The key to recognizing this as a multiplication problem is the word "of" in "I want $\frac{1}{3}$ *of* those dominoes." Those dominoes are $\frac{1}{2}$, so $\frac{1}{3} \times \frac{1}{2} = \frac{1}{6}$.

8. She uses $\frac{27}{32}$ of a gallon of glue and has $2\frac{17}{32}$ gallons left.

She uses $\frac{1}{4}$ of the glue, so you multiply $\frac{27}{8} \times \frac{1}{4} = \frac{27}{32}$. She uses $\frac{27}{32}$ of a gallon of glue. How much will she have left? Well, how much did she start with? $\frac{27}{8}$. So to find $\frac{27}{8} - \frac{27}{32}$, look at the denominators. Is one a multiple of the other? Sure, 32 is a multiple of 8. Multiply $\dfrac{27}{8}$ by $\dfrac{4}{4}$ and you get $\dfrac{108}{32}$. So $\dfrac{108}{32} - \dfrac{27}{32} = \dfrac{81}{32}$, or $2\dfrac{17}{32}$.

9. $\dfrac{32}{3}$ or $10\dfrac{2}{3}$

Taylor is separating his nails into smaller groups, which is known to the math-smart among us as dividing. He has $\dfrac{8}{3}$ buckets of nails and wants to divide the nails into buckets filled only $\dfrac{1}{4}$ of the way. So, $\dfrac{8}{3} \div \dfrac{1}{4} = \dfrac{8}{3} \times \dfrac{4}{1} = \dfrac{32}{3} = 10\dfrac{2}{3}$ of those $\dfrac{1}{4}$ filled buckets.

10. $\dfrac{115}{32}$ or $3\dfrac{19}{32}$

When you see the word "of," you have a multiplication question. So $5\dfrac{3}{4} \times \dfrac{3}{8} = \dfrac{23}{4} \times \dfrac{3}{8} = \dfrac{69}{32}$ and $5\dfrac{3}{4} - \dfrac{69}{32} = \dfrac{184}{32} - \dfrac{69}{32} = \dfrac{115}{32}$.

QUIZ # 5

DECIMALS

1. 200

The hundreds place is where the 2 is, and the number to the right of it is 3. Is 3 less than 5? It sure is, so the 2 remains a 2.

2. 13.5

The tenths place is just to the right of the decimal point, and the 5 to the right of the tenths place means that the 4 is rounded up 1.

3. 5.8

The numbers, when rounded, are 2.3 and 3.5, then 2.3+3.5=5.8 .

4. 3.534

Make sure to line up the decimal places exactly when you subtract.

5. 19.82

Did you approximate first? Then did you line up the numbers according to their decimal places?

6. 3

Look at 2.32. The tenths place is directly to the right of the decimal point. If you need a little help in visualizing, think about which place is the one that makes you think of dimes.

7. $6.29

Just line up the decimal places and add. 3.79+2.50=6.29

8. $0.34 or $\frac{34}{100}$ or $\frac{17}{50}$

Simple subtraction with decimals is just a matter of lining them up!

$2.32 - 1.98 = 0.34$. Since the decimal extends as far as the hundredths place, it is equal to $\frac{34}{100}$. Then you can reduce.

9. 2.356 grams

Amazing! The decimal gets shorter when you add! Of course, if you want you can leave that 0 on the end, but it isn't necessary.

10. 1.52 gallons

This was tough to get lined up unless you remembered to add the zeroes, especially when you are doing subtraction.
$4.30 - 2.78 = 1.52$.

MULTIPLYING AND DIVIDING DECIMALS

1. 9.2

Without decimals, 23×4 is 92, then move one space to the left for the one decimal place, and you have 9.2.

2. 1.7

Since you are dividing by 2, put the 3.4 under the division roof and put the decimal point on top, then divide.

$$
\begin{array}{r}
1.7 \\
2\overline{)3.4} \\
-2 \\
\hline
14 \\
-14 \\
\hline
0
\end{array}
$$

3. 6.72

Multiply without the decimal points and then count the number of places in the numbers being multiplied. Move the decimal that number of spaces from the right to the left of the product.

4. 2

Set up the division first. Then, move the decimal point of the number you are dividing by, in this case 0.9, to the right until it is a whole number, in this case 9. Then, move the decimal point of the number being divided into, in this case 1.8, the same number of spaces to the right. Then divide. Presto!

$$.9. \overline{)1.8.} \Rightarrow 9 \overline{)18}^{2}$$

5. 230

You could divide the same way you just did in question 4, or you could set this up as a fraction form of division. Move the decimal points over to make the 0.01 a whole number, just as you would in any other division set up, and you have $\dfrac{230}{1}$, better known as 230.

6. $13.60

If you approximated first, you would have an idea of what the final price should be. (Approximating is an excellent habit to get into.) What kind of problem is this? Multiplication. He does this four times.

$$3.4 \times 4 = 13.6$$

7. 2.6 ounces

What type of problem is this? Division, because he is separating the juice into two groups, also known as dividing it. So $5.2 \div 2 = 2.6$.

8. 14 groups

This is a division problem, and you can do it as decimal division.

$7 \div 0.5$ becomes $70 \div 5 = 14$, or convert the decimal to a fraction. $0.5 = \dfrac{5}{10} = \dfrac{1}{2}$, then $7 \div \dfrac{1}{2}$ becomes 7×2. Any way you slice it, the answer comes up as 14 piles of 50 cents each.

9. Jennifer receives 7.55 pounds of gelatin on an average day. (An accurate estimation could be between 6 and 9 pounds per day.)

This is another multiplication problem, because we are talking about how many *times* per day, and that *times* the gelatin per knockout will give you your answer. Was your approximation close to the right answer?

10. 9 teeny-tiny glasses! That is approximately 10 teeny-tiny glasses.

She is separating the one glassful into many smaller glasses. This means that she is dividing up the milk. So $0.45 \div 0.05$. Move the decimal in the 0.05 over to make it a whole number, move the one in 0.45 over the same amount, and go!

REVIEW

1. 6.3

   When you are adding decimals, be sure to align the digit places.

2. 0.8

   Did you approximate that the answer would be less than 1? Line them up and subtract, and then you're done.

3. 4.8

   Multiply as though there were no decimal and then count from the right of the product and put the decimal in.

4. 1.6

   Don't forget to place the decimal point in the division answer.

5. 4

   Either set up the equation as regular division and move the decimal point until the 0.6 becomes a whole number, or convert the decimals to fractions and divide the fractions the way you learned in chapter 3.

6. $3.00

   Just line up the decimals by the decimal places and add.
   $$\begin{array}{r} 2.55 \\ +0.45 \\ \hline \end{array}$$

7. $1.88

   Line up those digits and subtract away!

8. $2.10

This is actually a multiplication problem. One basket is 35 cents, 2 baskets are 2 times 35 cents, and so on. So $6 \times 0.35 = 210$. Move the decimal point over two spaces to the left because of the two decimal places in 0.35, and you have 2.10. Is that what you approximated?

9. 1121 grams

This multiplication problem is a lot like problem 8. So $2.3 \times 5 = 11.5$, and to express 11.5 as a mixed number, use the 11 as the whole number and convert the 0.5 to $\frac{5}{10}$ to $\frac{1}{2}$.

10. 12.7 piles

If Jennifer wants to divide the feathers, so do you. So $6.35 \div 0.5$; move the decimal point from 0.5 over 1 place to form a whole number and move the decimal point of the 6.35 over one place as well, and then divide.

PROPORTIONS AND RATIOS

1. 2 : 3

Both 4 and 6 are even, so they can be divided by 2. The ratio is then 2 : 3.

2. 12

Remember, in a proportion set up this way, the extremes will multiply to the same product as the means. So, $2 \times ?$ is equal to 3×8 means $2 \times ? = 24$. 24 divided by 2 is 12.

3. 15

Just cross-multiply when a proportion is set up this way. $4 \times ? = 5 \times 12$, so $4 \times ? = 60$. Divide both sides by 4. The missing piece is 15.

4. 8

Again, just cross-multiply. $3 \times ? = 4 \times 6$, so $3 \times ? = 24$, and 24 divided by 3 is 8.

5. 3.3

You can cross-multiply and find that $10 \times ? = 3 \times 11$, and 33 divided by 10 is 3.3.

6. 2 : 1

Careful, the question asks for the ratio of *compact discs* to *cassettes*, not the way it was originally given in the problem. The original was cassettes to CDs, or 4 : 8. Since you need to reverse it, it is 8 : 4, which reduces to 2 : 1.

7. 6 cups of water

You can use a ratio box for this.

	Sand	Water	Total Cement
	3	2	5
Multiply by	3	3	3
	9	6	15

Once you have found that the total of the ratio is 5 by adding the 2 parts and you know the real total is 15, you realize that the ratio was multiplied by 3. Thus, each part was multiplied by 3. Since there were 2 parts water, 3 times that is 6.

8. 9 tablespoons of flour

   The ratio of water to flour is 1 to 3. Add those parts and you have the total. You can use the ratio box.

	Water	Flour	Total
	1	3	4
Multiply by	3	3	3
	3	9	12

   The total is 4. It was multiplied by 3 to form 12 tablespoons, so the parts are multiplied by 3. Flour (3) is multiplied by 3 to become 9. Another way to do this problem is to ask yourself what fractional part of the whole the flour is. Since the whole of the ratio is 4 and the flour is 3 parts of that, the fractional part of the ratio is $\frac{3}{4}$. Of twelve cups, how much is flour? $\frac{3}{4} \times 12 = 9$.

9. 14

   Try the ratio box. The 2-to-1 ratio adds up to 3. What is 3 multiplied by to become 21? Yep, 7.

	Nonfiction	Fiction	Total
	1	2	3
Multiplied by	7	7	7
	7	14	21

The 2 parts that are fiction books are also multiplied by 7 to become 14. Could you have done this by transforming the ratio into a fraction? Sure, $\dfrac{3}{2} = \dfrac{21}{14}$.

10. 4 gallons of hot fudge

Try a ratio box. You multiply the total number of gallons by 4 to get the 16 gallons, so the 1 part fudge is also multiplied by 4.

QUIZ # 9

CONVERSION

1. 0.5 and 50%

2. 0.75 and 75%

    Just multiply 3 by $\dfrac{25}{25}$ to get $\dfrac{75}{100}$.

3. $\dfrac{2}{5}$ (reduced from $\dfrac{4}{10}$) and 40%

4. 0.3 and $\dfrac{3}{10}$

5. 0.2 and $\dfrac{1}{5}$ (reduced from $\dfrac{2}{10}$)

6. 0.29 and $\dfrac{29}{100}$

7. 0.7 and 70%

    Remember, if the decimal only extends to the tenths place, just add a 0 into the hundredths place for your percentage.

8. 0.06 and 6%

This becomes $\dfrac{6}{100}$, so the 6 goes in the hundredths place and a 0 goes in the tenths place.

9. $\dfrac{23}{100}$ and 23%

10. $\dfrac{1}{1000}$ and 0.1%

To transform a decimal to a percent, move the decimal point two spaces over to the right and add a percent sign. All it means here is that you have a fractional percentage.

QUIZ # 10

PERCENTAGES

1. 5

To find 10% of a number, just move the decimal point of that number one space to the left.

2. 4

You can easily reduce 25% to $\dfrac{25}{100}$ to $\dfrac{1}{4}$, and then multiply as you would a fraction.

$\dfrac{1}{4} \times 16 = 4$.

3. 9

You can transform the percentage to a fraction, cancel if possible, and then multiply. $\dfrac{3}{\underset{1}{\cancel{100}}} \times \dfrac{\overset{3}{\cancel{300}}}{1} = \dfrac{9}{1} = 9$

4. 46

You can cross-multiply: 2,300 = 50 × ? Then divide both sides by 50. ? = 46

Another way to look at it is to think about equal fractions. 50 was multiplied by 2, to make 100, so you must multiply 23 by 2 as well.

5. 8

Well, you have a lot of different options to solve this problem. You could change $\frac{2}{25}$ to $\frac{2}{25} \times \frac{4}{4} = \frac{8}{100}$, which is 8%, or you could cross-multiply.

6. 1

Careful! The question wants to know how many she has *left*, not how many she gave away. You could find 90% of 10, which is 9, and then subtract 9 from 10, which means 1 left. Or, since she gave away 90%, she kept 10%. What is 10% of 10? Move the decimal point over one space to the left: 10% of 10 is 1.

7. $384

Set up your multiplication when you see the word *of*.

$$\frac{32}{100} \times 1200 = 384$$

8. 0

Aren't you shocked? Taylor, who is so sweet to his friends, turns out to be an utter creep when he deals with his brother. Well, maybe he's not a total creep. If his brother is math-smart at all, he knows that anything times 0—and "of" means times—is 0.

9. 10%

You can set this up as a proportion, then cross-multiply. $\dfrac{3}{30} = \dfrac{?}{100}$

Or you can reduce $\dfrac{3}{30}$, to make life easier, to $\dfrac{1}{10}$. And $\dfrac{1}{10}$ is 10%.

10. 0.5% or $\dfrac{1}{2}$ %

Tricky question! Did you get caught? Set the question up as a proportion, then cross-multiply. $\dfrac{1}{200} = \dfrac{?}{100}$, so $200 \times ? = 1 \times 100$. You get $\dfrac{1}{2}$, so the answer is one-half of a percent.

QUIZ # 11

REVIEW

1. $\dfrac{1}{5}$ and 0.2

The decimal part is easy. Move the decimal two places to the left and drop the percent sign. Then you can set up 20% as a fraction over 100, as all percents are, and reduce.

$$20\% = \dfrac{20}{100} = \dfrac{1}{5}$$

2. 12

Cross-multiply. $24 = 2 \times ?$ Two times 12 is 24.

3. 6

A proportion has extremes (the outsides) that multiply to the same product as the means (the insides). $1 \times ? = 2 \times 3$ so $? = 6$.

4. 0.25 and 25%

First, transform $\frac{1}{4}$ into a fraction over 100.

$$\frac{1}{4} \times \frac{25}{25} = \frac{25}{100}$$

Since the number now has a denominator of 100, you can put it in the hundredths place of the decimal (0.25) move the decimal two to the right, and add a percentage sign for the percent.

5. 0.15 and 15%

First it becomes a fraction with a denominator of 100, $\frac{15}{100}$, then it easily becomes a decimal in the hundredths place, and then a percentage.

6. 15 cups of ink, and the mixture is 60% ink

Setting up a ratio box is probably your best bet here.

	Water	Ink	Total
	2	3	5
Multiply by	5	5	5
	10	15	25

The total writing mixture has 5 parts, which were then multiplied by 5 to become 25 cups. Thus, the ink part is multiplied by 5, and 3 × 5 = 15. To find the percentage, you can look to the original ratio. If the ink to water ratio is 3 : 2, then the total is 5 and the part that is ink is 3. So $\dfrac{3}{5}$ is the fractional part of the mixture that is ink, and

$$\dfrac{3}{5} \times \dfrac{20}{20} = \dfrac{60}{100} = 60\%$$

7. 28 marbles

   You can set this up as a regular multiplication problem.
   $14\% \times 200 = 0.14 \times 200 = 28$.

8. 12 pints of red food coloring; yellow is 25% of the mixture.

   First, you can set up a ratio box, with the ratio of red to yellow at 3 to 1, and the total at 4.

	Red	Yellow	Total
	3	1	4
Multiply by	4	4	4
	12	4	16

   Since you want the real total to be 16, you multiply each part by 4, and the 3 red parts become 12. To find the yellow percentage, just use fractional parts from the ratio. The ratio is 3 : 1 red to yellow, so 4 is the total and there is $\dfrac{1}{4}$ yellow in the whole. $\dfrac{1}{4} = 25\%$. You can also remember that $\dfrac{1}{4}$ is one quarter, also known among those who carry money as $0.25. Cool, huh?

9. 1 : 1

Percent, you ask? Well, fifty-fifty means $\frac{1}{2}$ water and $\frac{1}{2}$ salt. So the parts are each 1 and the whole is 2, so the ratio is 1 : 1, adding up to a whole of 2.

10. 3

You can use a ratio box again, but you don't know the real whole number, just the real number of cars.

	Cars	Trucks	Total
	5	1	6
Multiply by	3	3	3
	15	3	18

That means the real number of cars is 15, so the 5 parts were multiplied by 3. Multiply everything else by 3 and you have 3 trucks, and a total of 18 vehicles in the set.

PROBABILITY

1. $\frac{1}{5}$

Probability is determined by the number of successful possibilities over the number of total possibilities. So 1 green over the 5 total possibilities is $\frac{1}{5}$.

2. $\dfrac{2}{5}$

You should use the same reasoning as in question 1. In this question, though, the red jellybean is more likely, as there are 2 reds and only 1 green.

3. 0

It is absolutely certain that you will not select a white jellybean as there are none in the bag, so the probability is $\dfrac{0}{5}$ or 0.

4. $\dfrac{1}{25}$

This is a little more difficult. To find out how many possibilities there are for two events, you multiply the number of possibilities. So there are 5 different possibilities for the first and 5 for the second, and 5 × 5 = 25. There is only 1 way to get 2 greens, so $\dfrac{1}{25}$.

5. $\dfrac{4}{25}$

The probability for orange the first time is $\dfrac{2}{5}$, then for the second is $\dfrac{2}{5}$ again. To find the probability of both, multiply and you get $\dfrac{4}{25}$. You can write out the possibilities to check yourself, if you'd like.

6. $\dfrac{4}{25}$

The probability that the first jellybean will be red is $\dfrac{2}{5}$, and since you put it back before picking the second one, the probability of red for the second jellybean is also $\dfrac{2}{5}$. Multiply $\dfrac{2}{5} \times \dfrac{2}{5} = \dfrac{4}{25}$.

7. $\dfrac{1}{25}$

You can do this one just like the last one, but the probability is only $\dfrac{1}{5}$ for each draw because there is only 1 green jellybean. $\dfrac{1}{5} \times \dfrac{1}{5} = \dfrac{1}{25}$.

8. $\dfrac{1}{10}$

The probability that the first jellybean is orange is $\dfrac{2}{5}$. Since you don't put the first jellybean back, there are only 4 jellybeans left, and if the first jellybean you drew was orange, there is only 1 orange left. That means that the probability that the second jellybean will be orange is $\dfrac{1}{4}$. Multiply $\dfrac{2}{5} \times \dfrac{1}{4} = \dfrac{2}{20} = \dfrac{1}{10}$.

9. $\dfrac{1}{10}$

The probability of pulling a green on the first draw is $\dfrac{1}{5}$, because there is 1 green among the 5, and the probability of pulling a red on the second draw is $\dfrac{2}{4}$, because there are 2 reds among the 4 jellybeans left in the bag. $\dfrac{1}{5} \times \dfrac{2}{4} = \dfrac{2}{20} = \dfrac{1}{10}$.

10. 0

The probability of pulling a green on the first draw is $\frac{1}{5}$, but if that first 1 is green and you don't put it back, there are no greens left for the second draw. $\frac{1}{5} \times 0 = 0$.

PERMUTATIONS AND COMBINATIONS

1. 6

You can list these out easily. Or you can say, "How many possibilities for the first one? Three. How many for the second? Two. For the third? One." Then multiply.

$$3 \times 2 \times 1 = 6$$

2. 12

Again, either list or use the math you've learned. How many prizes can be the first prize on the wall? Four. The second? Three. Multiply.

$$4 \times 3 = 12$$

3. 12

How many possibilities for engines? Three. How many hull designs? Two. How many interior designs? Two. Then multiply.

$$3 \times 2 \times 2 = 12$$

4. 12

Eerie! Soon you will think all the answers to combination questions are 12, but it isn't true. Just see how many possibilities there are for each stage: fruit, two; bread, three; cheese, two. Multiply.

$$2 \times 3 \times 3 = 12$$

5. 720

That is a lot of possible combinations; be glad that you don't have to make the decision. You are back to arrangements of possibilities or permutations. How many could be the first move? Ten. The second has nine possibilities, since you have used one of the moves up on the first, and the third has eight, since you have used two of the moves on the first two of the sequence. $10 \times 9 \times 8 = 720$.

AVERAGE, MEDIAN, AND MODE

1. 3

You can add them up and divide by 3 because there are 3 numbers. $2 + 3 + 4 = 9$, then $9 \div 3 = 3$. But you also might want to notice a nice trick: In any odd-numbered group of consecutive numbers, the average (mean) of the group is the number directly in the middle.

2. 5

Add the 2 numbers and then divide by 2. $3 + 7 = 10$. $10 \div 2 = 5$.

3. 4

Add them up then divide by 5, as there are 5 numbers in the group.

4. 3

Line them up in size order: 1, 3, 3, 6, 7. Which number is in the exact middle? 3.

5. 3

The mode is the number that occurs most frequently. Since 3 appears twice and the other numbers only appear once each, 3 is the mode.

6. 8

To find the average, add up the numbers and divide by how many there are. Here, 3 + 6 + 15 = 24, then 24 divided by 3, the number of days, is 8.

7. 12

You know how to find the average; just add the numbers and divide by how many days there are. So you get 36 divided by 3, which is 12. Now, to find the approximate average for Thursday and Saturday, look at the numbers from those days: 10 and 14. Just to approximate, it doesn't look as though their average would be all that different from 12, and it isn't. If you bother to check, you can find that the average of Thursday and Saturday is exactly 12.

8. $4

Add them all, and don't forget that when it says "Two of them are 3 dollars each," you must add the 3 dollars twice. $2 + $3 + $3 + $4 + $4 + $8 = $24. Divide $24 by 6 to get an average of $4.

9. 4

You can use your incredible multiplication skills here. Three 8-person families is just 3 times 8, or 24, and 4 one-person families are just 4 people. Add them up and you have 28. Because the question says "7 houses," you can just divide the 28 by 7 to get 4.

10. Average: 24 inches

Mode: 20 inches

Median: 25 inches

To find the average, add the jump heights then divide by how many jumps there were, which is 5 in this case. Then determine the mode. List the numbers and find the one that occurs most. You might as well list them in size order because you will have to find the median next: 20, 20, 25, 26, 29. The number that occurs most frequently is 20, so that is the mode. The median is the number smack dab in the middle, and that is 25.

QUIZ # 15

REVIEW

1. 0

There are no green marbles, so it is certain that Rose will not choose one. The way to express the certainty that an event will not happen is that it has a probability of $\frac{0}{20}$, or 0.

2. $\dfrac{3}{20}$

The number of successful possibilities is 3 for the 3 blue marbles. The number of total possibilities is 20 for the 20 marbles in the bag.

3. $\dfrac{2}{19}$

Since Rose is not replacing the marbles, the draws are dependent. The probability that the first marble will be green is $\dfrac{10}{20}$. For the second draw, there are 19 marbles, of which 9 are green, so the probability is $\dfrac{9}{19}$. On the final try, there are 8 green marbles out of 18 remaining. Multiply $\dfrac{10}{20} \times \dfrac{9}{19} \times \dfrac{8}{18} = \dfrac{1}{2} \times \dfrac{9}{19} \times \dfrac{8^4}{18_2} = \dfrac{4}{38} = \dfrac{2}{19}$.

4. $\dfrac{1}{2}$

You can reduce probabilities. There is a total of 10 balls, and the number of successful possibilities is 5, so $\dfrac{5}{10}$ or $\dfrac{1}{2}$. The two probabilities are equal.

5. 1

Since there are only blue balls in the box, the number of successful outcomes is the same as the number of possible outcomes, or $\dfrac{10}{10}$, which equals 1. A probability of 1 means the successful outcome is certain.

6. 53 inches

Add the numbers together and divide by how many numbers there were (in this case, three years).

$159 \div 3 = 53$

Did you also notice that 53 is exactly in the middle of an odd group of numbers? You just could have chosen it as the average if you thought of it, and it is often nice to do less work than you might to get the same answer.

7. 18

Again, here the numbers are an odd group in exact order, so you can choose the middle number. Or you can add them and divide by how many there are.

$16 + 18 + 20 = 54$, and $54 \div 3 = 18$.

8. 210

This is a permutation question, so you need to figure out the arrangements. How many possibilities are there for the first song on the tape? Well, there are 7 songs on the tape, so there are 7 possibilities for the first song. There are 6 songs left possible for the second, and 5 songs left after that for the third song. Multiply.

$7 \times 6 \times 5 = 210$

9. Mean: 21 minutes per mile

Mode: 20 minutes per mile

Median: 20 minutes per mile

For the mean, add them up and divide. $20 + 23 + 20 + 24 + 18 = 105$, and $105 \div 5 = 21$.

For the mode, list them in order as well so the median is easier, and find the one that occurs most frequently: 18, 20, 20, 23, 24. Twenty occurs most frequently and is smack dab in the middle as well, so it is the median as well as the mode.

10. $\dfrac{1}{81}$

Because Jennifer replaces the marble after she picks one up, there is always a probability of $\dfrac{1}{3}$. So to find the series of probabilities, multiply these. $\dfrac{1}{3} \times \dfrac{1}{3} \times \dfrac{1}{3} \times \dfrac{1}{3} = \dfrac{1}{81}$. It isn't all that likely, is it?

QUIZ # 16

READING LINE GRAPHS

1. 20

Look above 1994 until you see the point and then move sideways to the left axis. The number there is 20, and that is how many people learned to dive that year.

2. 2000

The highest point of the graph gives the greatest number of people, and that is 35 people in 2000.

3. 1992

   Look for the lowest point on the graph. It's all the way to the left, in 1992.

4. 1995–1996

   You are looking for the steepest rise from left to right, and it is between 1995 and 1996. You can also subtract year to year if you aren't sure.

5. 1994–1995

   Now you are looking for the steepest decline from left to right, which is between 1994 and 1995. You can subtract again and look for the greatest difference if you like.

READING PICTOGRAPHS

1. 200

   Since each symbol represents 100 people and there are two farmer symbols, the pictograph indicates that there are 200 farmers who like music in Smalltown.

2. 400

   Each symbol is 100, and there are 4 of them for the teachers, so 400 teachers like music.

3. There are more teachers.

   You know from questions 1 and 2 that there are 400 teachers and 200 farmers who like music, so there are more teachers in this graph, but bear in mind that this does not mean that teachers in general like music more, even in Smalltown. Why? Because it is possible that there are only 200 farms, so all the farmers like music, and it is also possible that there are 2,000 teachers, so only 10% of the teachers in Smalltown like music. With this pictograph, you cannot tell.

4. There are more athletes.

   There are 2 athlete symbols, or 200 athletes who like music in Smalltown, and only 1 cowboy symbol, or only 100 cowboys in Smalltown who like music.

5. Students

   There are 5 student symbols, or 500 students in Smalltown who like to listen to music, more than any of the other groups represented.

QUIZ # 18

READING CIRCLE GRAPHS

1. There are more black widows.

   How do you know? Look at the chart; the section taken up by black widows is larger. Now look at the numbers: the collection is 23% black widows, compared to 20% water spiders.

2. There are more tarantulas.

   Again, look at the graph and see which section is bigger, or which percentage—37% or 15%—is bigger. Clearly, 37% is a greater portion of the collection.

3. 23

   Well, if the whole is 100, and 23% of the whole is black widow spiders, to find the actual number of black widows, remember percent means out of 100. You would also do well to remember that when you are asked to find a certain percent of 100, since percent just means per 100, the answer is the number of the percent. In other words, 23% of 100 is 23, and 5% of 100 is 5, and so on.

4. 20

   Since water spiders are 20% of the whole and the whole is 100, there are 20 water spiders in the collection.

5. 63

   There are many ways to answer this question. Some of you may have added up all the other percents and gotten 63, and that's terrific. Another quicker way is to simply subtract the tarantulas from the whole. So the whole is 100, there are 37 tarantulas, and that leaves 63 other spiders.

REVIEW

1. 100

   Look at the 1965 line, go up to the point, and then look over to the left to the number of people.

2. 250

   If you got somewhere between 200 and 260, that is close enough; when you have question on a year that is not represented clearly, look at your graph and approximate.

3. Any year between 1987–1990

   The highest point on the graph is at 1987–1990, so those are the years in which the greatest number of people knew how to hula hoop.

4. 1980–1985

   The steepest rise occurs between 1980 and 1985, when there was an increase of approximately 200 people.

5. 100

   Since each symbol represents 100 people and there is 1 symbol for the bowlers, 100 bowlers like coconut.

6. 400

   Four tennis racket symbols represent 400 people.

7. 500

There are 6 symbols for basketball players and one symbol for bowlers, so the difference is 5 symbols, which represent 500 people.

8. Reading

Reading accounts for 12% of her free time, while spacing out only accounts for 8% of her free time. Therefore, reading accounts for more of her free time.

9. 6 hours

You need to find 12% of the whole, or 12% of 50.

$$\frac{12}{{}_{2}\cancel{100}} \times \frac{\cancel{50}^{1}}{1} = \frac{12}{2} = 6$$

10. 5 hours

Combining the 2 activities from the start will be easiest. They account for 10% of the whole. Since the whole is 50, you can take 10% easily by moving the decimal point one space to the left and getting 5.

QUIZ # 20

POINTS, LINES AND ANGLES

1. $\overleftrightarrow{EF}$ or $\overleftrightarrow{GJ}$ or $\overleftrightarrow{KN}$ or $\overleftrightarrow{PS}$

There are four lines in the picture. Look for the ones with arrows on both ends. You can name the line by any two points on the line, so $\overleftrightarrow{GJ}$, $\overleftrightarrow{HJ}$, and $\overrightarrow{GH}$ are all possible names for the same line. Remember to put the line symbol on top of the two letters.

2. $\overline{JM}$

$\overline{JM}$ is the segment that connects point *J* to point *M*. You could also name any part of one of the lines, by naming two points on the line and putting the segment symbol over the top, for example, $\overline{HL}$.

3. $\overrightarrow{ST}$

A ray has one endpoint and goes on forever in the other direction. You could also choose a point on a line to be the endpoint of a ray, and a second point to tell what direction the ray is going, for example, $\overrightarrow{QE}$. Don't forget to put the ray symbol on top.

4. Point *S*

You don't even need to look at the picture. When an angle is named with three letters, the middle letter is the vertex.

5. $\overrightarrow{ST}$ and $\overrightarrow{SR}$

The sides of an angle are rays that have the vertex as their endpoint. One side goes from *S* through *T*, and the other from *S* through *R*.

6. ∠RST, ∠HJM, or ∠JMN

Look for an angle that is smaller than a right angle. Remember acute comes to a sharp point.

7. ∠JML

Obtuse angles are larger than a right angle. There are other angles that might be obtuse, but there aren't enough letters on the picture to let us name them.

8. $\overrightarrow{JG} \perp \overleftrightarrow{FE}$ or $\overleftrightarrow{NK} \perp \overleftrightarrow{FE}$ or $\overleftrightarrow{SP} \perp \overleftrightarrow{FE}$

Each of these pairs of lines looks perpendicular, but we can be certain about $\overrightarrow{JG} \perp \overleftrightarrow{FE}$ because the right angle is marked.

9. $\angle$FHG

You can be sure that $\angle$FHG is a right angle because it has the square marking it. Several other angles look like right angles. Remember that perpendicular lines form right angles.

10. $\overleftrightarrow{KN} \parallel \overleftrightarrow{PS}$, $\overleftrightarrow{KN} \parallel \overrightarrow{GJ}$, or $\overrightarrow{GJ} \parallel \overleftrightarrow{PS}$

As best we can tell by looking, these lines will never meet.

POLYGONS AND CIRCLES

Use the drawing to answer the questions below.

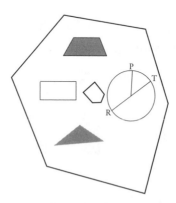

1. Hexagon

A polygon with six sides is called a hexagon.

2. Pentagon

   This one has five sides, so it's a pentagon.

3. 107°

   The three angles of the triangle must add up to 180°. The two we know about add up to 31 + 42 = 73°, so the third one must be 180 − 73 = 107°.

4. Obtuse

   In question 3, you found out the triangle contains an angle of 107°, so the triangle is an obtuse triangle.

5. 125°

   The four angles of a quadrilateral will add to 360°. Add up the ones you know. 60° + 120° + 55° = 235°. Subtract from 360° to find the fourth angle. 360° − 235° = 125°.

6. No, it's not a parallelogram. It's a trapezoid.

   This quadrilateral has one pair of parallel sides, not two. To be a parallelogram, it would have to have two pairs of parallel sides.

7. Yes, they are congruent.

   The triangles seem to be the same shape and size. They look like copies of one another, so they are congruent.

8. No, they are not similar.

   To be similar, they would have to be the same shape, but different sizes. These quadrilaterals are not the same shape.

9. Radius could be $\overline{OP}$, $\overline{OR}$, or $\overline{OT}$. The diameter is $\overline{RT}$.

A radius is a line segment that connects the center O to a point on the circle. A diameter has both ends on the circle.

10. 4π or approximately 12.56

The circumference of a circle is the diameter times π. Use 3.14 as an approximate value for π, and multiply $3.14 \times 4 = 12.56$.

QUIZ # 22

PERIMETER AND AREA

1. 144 square meters

Area of a square is side squared, so 12 meters $\times$ 12meters = 144 square meters.

2. 48 meters

Each of the four sides is 12 meters long. Add them up—or multiply 4 $\times$ 12 meters = 48 meters.

3. 46 feet

Two sides measure 18 feet and two sides measure 5 feet. Add them up. 18 feet +18 feet + 5 feet + 5 feet = 46 feet

4. 90 square feet

Area of a rectangle is length times width or base times height. 18 feet $\times$ 5 feet = 90 square feet.

5. The area of a triangle is equal to $\frac{1}{2}bh = \frac{1}{2} \times 194$ centimeters $\times 22$ centimeters = 2134 square centimeters

6. 36 square inches

   The area of a parallelogram is base times height = 9 inches $\times$ 4 inches = 36 square inches.

7. Area = 126 square feet. Perimeter = 46 feet.

   Area =14 feet $\times$ 9 feet wide = 126 square feet. Perimeter = 2 $\times$ 14 feet + 2 $\times$ 9 feet = 46 feet.

8. 160 square feet

   The area of a trapezoid is $\frac{1}{2}$ the sum of the bases times the height. The bases add to 13 feet + 19 feet = 32 feet. Half of that is 16 feet. Multiply that by the height of 10 feet and you get 160 square feet.

9. 6.5π or approximately 20.41 inches.

   The circumference of a circle is π times the diameter. Use 3.14 as an approximate value of π. 6.5 inches $\times$ 3.14 = approximately 20.41 inches.

10. Approximately 33.17 square inches

    The area of a circle is π times the square of the radius. The radius is half the diameter. Half of 6.5 inches is 3.25 inches. 3.25 inches, squared, is 10.5625 square inches. Use 3.14 as an approximate value of π. 10.5625 square inches $\times$ 3.14 = 33.16625 square inches. Round to the nearest hundredth, and you get approximately 33.17 square inches.

THE PYTHAGOREAN THEOREM

1. 13 cm

   $5^2 = 25$ and $12^2 = 144$. Add them together and you get $25 + 144 = 169$. What number can you square to get 169? It's bigger than 12, but not a lot bigger. Experiment a little and you'll find it's 13.

2. 10 feet

   You can do the work out if you want. $6^2 + 8^2 = 36 + 64 = 100$, which is 10 squared. Or you can notice that 6 is 2 times 3 and 8 is 2 times 4, and remember that a triangle with legs of 3 and 4 has a hypotenuse of 5. So a triangle with legs of 2 times 3 and 2 times 4 has a hypotenuse of 2 times 5, or 10.

3. 130 inches

   $50 = 5 \times 10$ and $120 = 12 \times 10$, so look back to question 1 and use the shortcut. The hypotenuse is 13×10 or 130. (Or you can do the work out. $502 + 1202 = 2500 + 14400 = 16900$. What squares to 16900? 130!)

4. 50 miles
   $30^2 + 40^2 = 900 + 1600 = 2500$, and $2500 = 50^2$. (Or us the shortcut.)

5. 65 meters
   $25 = 5 \times 5$ and $60 = 12 \times 5$ so the hypotenuse will be $13 \times 5 = 65$.

3-DIMENSIONAL FIGURES AND VOLUME

1. Cylinder

2. Cube and Cylinder

3. Volume is 288 cubic feet

   Volume = length times width times height, so $4 \times 9 \times 8 = 288$ cubic feet.

4. 2.16 pounds

   The volume of the box is 18 inches $\times$ 10 inches $\times$ 6 inches = 1080 cubic inches. If 500 cubic inches of jellybeans weigh 1 pound, 1080 cubic inches will be more than 2 pounds. To find out exactly how much, divide 1080 cubic inches by 500 cubic inches. $1080 \div 500 = 2.16$ pounds.

5. 0.24 pounds less

   The volume of Jennifer's box is 24 inches $\times$ 8 inches $\times$ 5 inches = 960 cubic inches, so she has less room to hold jellybeans. 960 cubic inches $\div$ 500 cubic inches = 1.92 pounds. Subtract to find out how much less she has. 2.16 pounds – 1.92 pounds = 0.24 pounds. Jennifer will have just a little less than a quarter of a pound less than Taylor.

REVIEW

1. Square

   Squares have four equal sides.

2. Hexagon

   Hexagons have six sides, and they are closed and flat.

3. The diameter

4. 30 degrees, which means it is an acute angle.

   One way to make approximating easier is to imagine a perpendicular line—that is, a line forming a right angle—extending from the bottom of the angle and compare the angle in question to the right angle. First, is it larger or smaller than the right angle? This one is smaller, so it is acute. Is it less than half or more than half of a right angle? This one looks to be less than half, so it is less than 45. It looks to be around 30.

5. 24 cubic units

   The formula to find the volume of a rectangular solid is $l \times w \times h$. Since the length here is 2, the width is 4, and the height is 3, $2 \times 3 \times 4$ gives the volume, which is 24.

6. 26

   Add up the sides of the carpet, also known as the perimeter, and you get 26.

7. 8

Look at all the marked right angles. Did you notice the upside-down one? An angle has the same measurement no matter how it is oriented in space.

8. 6 square feet

You need to find the area that needs to be covered. Here the shape is a rectangle, so the area is the measure of the length times the width, or 2 times 3, which is 6.

9. The best way to describe it would be to call it a cone resting on its base, with a sphere balanced on top.

10. 4π

This question is asking you to find the circumference of the circle. The formula for circumference of a circle is pi times the diameter, or πd. Since the diameter—the line from edge to edge running through the middle—is 4, the circumference is 4π.

NEGATIVE NUMBERS

1. −5 is bigger

Look at a number line. Which one is closer to the positive numbers?

2. 0 is bigger

   Look at a number line again; 0 is closer to positive than –1, so it is bigger. Or think of it like this: If you have no money but don't owe anyone money, either, that's better than owing someone a dollar.

3. –13 is bigger

   It can get confusing because in the set of positive numbers, 31 would be bigger than 13, but with negative numbers everything is reversed. Think of debt again. The more you owe, the less you have.

4. –7

   What if you dug down 3 feet and then dug another 4? You would be 7 feet deep.

5. –12

6. –3

   Start at the positive number on the number line and then go down (as if you were digging a hole) 15 spaces for the –15. You go down past 0 to –3.

7. 1

   There are many ways to look at this. You can go on the number line to –3, and then, since you are subtracting a negative number, move up 4 spaces. When subtracting a negative you can combine the two minus signs to form a plus, so it's as though $-3 - -4 = ?$ really says $-3 + 4 = ?$

8. 18

Again, subtracting a negative is like adding a positive, so 8 − −10 can be rewritten as 8 + 10.

9. −5

Start at 12 on the number line and move down 17 spaces. You end up at −5. Or for a quick fix, just reverse the numbers and add a negative sign to the difference. 12 − 17 becomes 17 − 12 = 5, so the answer is −5.

10. 5

Subtracting a negative is like adding a positive, so 3 − −2 becomes 3 + 2, which is equal to 5.

MULTIPLYING AND DIVIDING NEGATIVE NUMBERS

1. −12

A negative times a positive is a negative.

2. 22

A negative times a negative is a positive.

3. 64

4. 0

   Anything, whether positive or negative, times 0 is equal to 0.

5. –20

6. 22

   A negative divided by a negative yields a positive.

7. –5

   A positive number divided by a negative number will give a negative number as the answer.

8. –4

9. 0

   Zero divided by any number, negative or positive, is equal to 0. If you have nothing to divide up, how many piles will you divide it into? None!

10. 2

   What is a negative number divided by a negative number? Positive, of course.

REVIEW

1. −1

   Just do it one step at a time and remember PEMDAS. First, parentheses.

   $3 + {-4}(2 - 1) =$

   $3 - 4(1) =$

   Since there are no exponents, any multiplication or division gets done left to right.

   $3 - 4(1) =$

   $3 - 4 = -1$. Use your number line if you like.

2. −14

   Since there is only addition and subtraction here, you do this problem left to right. Start at −5, then subtract 7, so go down 7 to −12, and then subtract another 2, so go down to −14.

3. −4

   This problem contains only multiplication and division, which you know from PEMDAS is done left to right. So −6 divided by −3 is 2, then 2 times −2 is equal to −4.

4. 0

   Left to right, you're just bouncing back and forth on the number line. Any number plus itself in the negative form is equal to 0, right? 5 +

–5, or –6 + 6. How else could you write this problem? How about 2(–1 + 1) because you do the same operation two times!

5. –3

Bring out your old pal PEMDAS and get to work. What is first? Why, parentheses, of course.

–2(–3 + –4) – 17 =

–2(–7) – 17

Next is multiplication, which leaves you with this.

14 – 17 =

You can now just reverse them and add on a negative sign, or move it onto the number line to see what happens. Think about it—the 14 and –14 of the –17 cancel each other out, and all you are left with is the extra –3 from the –17.

6. 12

Perform the division first, which gives you 5, then 5 plus 7 is 12.

7. –80

Multiplication and division go straight from left to right, so –32 times 5 is –160, divided by 2 is –80.

8. 35

This problem seems complicated, but it's simple once you break it down into steps. First, do the parentheses.

$$17 + 23 - -5(2 - 3) =$$

$$17 + 23 - -5(-1) =$$

Then do any multiplication or division.

$$17 + 23 - 5 =$$

That works because −5 times −1 becomes a positive. Now the addition and subtraction is straight left to right.

9. −1

Switch those babies around and add a negative sign.

10. 71

Subtracting a negative is like adding a positive. You are getting rid of debt, or filling up a hole, or however you want to view it. So put those two signs together to form a plus sign and add the numbers.

ALGEBRA

1. 4

2. 2

3. 6

4. 6

This is exactly the same expression as in question 3. The parentheses aren't written (because mathematicians can be lazy too), but you should know when you see $2x$ that it can be thought of as $2(x)$.

5. −3

   −*x* is exactly the same as −1*x* is exactly the same as −1 times *x*. They all mean the same thing.

6. −4

   Remember, −2 − 2 = −4. How much is −2 *times* −2? Positive 4.

7. 6

   A negative times a negative is always a positive.

8. 4

   Plug in −2 for the variables and you should get this: −8 − (−12). That's the same as −8 + 12, which of course gives 4 as the answer.

9. 7

   If *x* = 12, then *x* + 9 = 21. 21 divided by 3 is 7.

10. 9

   Remember PEMDAS! Parentheses first: *x* + 3 = 15. That negative sign outside the parentheses turns (15) into −15. Multiplication comes next: 2 × 12 = 24. Now the problem is simply 24 − 15.

EQUATIONS

1. $x = 4$

   All you needed to do was *subtract* 3 from *both* sides of the equation.

2. $x = 10$

   Add 9 to both sides of the equation.

3. $x = 4$

   Divide both sides of the equation by 3.

4. $x = 4$

   Divide both sides of the equation by -3. -3 divided by -3 is 1, because a negative divided by a negative is positive and the threes cancel out. -12 divided by -3 is the same as 12 divided by 3, which is 4. Again, because both numbers are negative and we're doing multiplication or division, the answer is positive.

5. $x = 1$

   Combine the two x's. $x + x$ is $2x$. $2x + 2 = 4$. Subtract 2 from both sides. (Remember, adding or subtracting is the next step.) Then divide both sides by 2. There you have $\frac{2}{2} = x$. $\frac{2}{2}$ is the same as 1, because any number divided by itself equals 1.

6. $x = 3$

   Combine $+3x$ with $-x$. That's $2x$. Now subtract seven from both sides. That leaves $2x = 6$. Divide both sides by 2. x does indeed equal 3.

7. $x = 12$

   Remember to multiply both sides by the denominator first. (Because there's nothing to combine, or you'd combine first.) That leaves $3x = 36$. Now it's simple. Divide both sides by 3.

8. $x = 2$

   Again, there's nothing to combine. This one's tricky. Multiply both sides by x. That leaves $20 = 10x$. On the left side the x's cancel; on the right side x times 10 is $10x$. Now divide both sides by 10.

9. $x = \dfrac{1}{4}$

   Start by subtracting 4 from each side. That leaves $\dfrac{7}{2x} = 14$. Multiply both sides by $2x$. That leaves $7 = 28x$. Divide both sides by 28. That leaves $\dfrac{7}{28} = x$, and $\dfrac{7}{28}$ reduces to $\dfrac{1}{4}$.

10. $x = 3$

    Combine first. The fractions can be added because they have the same denominator. So combined, the value is $\dfrac{11x}{3} = 11$. Now multiply both sides by 3. That leaves $11x = 33$. Divide both sides by 11. There you go. You're left with 30.

    Great job!

ADDITION REVIEW

1. 44

2. 34

3. 612

4. 399

5. 4,657

6. 35

   Well, 13 kittens plus 22 kittens is the same as 13 + 22, and 13 + 22 = 35.

7. 141 race cars

   Remember, the word "altogether" should have tipped you off that this was an addition problem. 28 + 113 = 41

8. 28 days absent.

   2 + 17 + 9 = 28. You might find it easier to rearrange: 2 + 9 + 17 = 11 + 17 = 28.

9. 148 stamps

   32 + 49 + 67 = 148

10. 323 sea shells

    12 + 31 + 17 + 263 = 323

SUBTRACTION REVIEW

1. 15

2. 33

3. 112

You had to borrow here.

$$
\begin{array}{r}
1\,{}^{2}\!\!\not{3}\,{}^{1}1 \\
-\ \ 1\ 9 \\
\hline
1\ \ 1\ \ 2
\end{array}
$$

4. 105

You had to borrow here too.

$$
\begin{array}{r}
1\not{3}\,{}^{1}4 \\
-\ \ 2\ 9 \\
\hline
1\ \ 0\ \ 5
\end{array}
$$

5. 894

Did you approximate first and realize that the answer had to be around 900? The borrowing is tough because of the zeros, so go all the way over to the 1 thousand, borrow it and change it to 10 hundreds. Borrow one of those hundreds and make it 10 tens. Borrow one of those tens and make it 10 ones. Then (finally!) you can subtract.

$$1001 \atop -107 \Rightarrow \quad {}^{0}\!\!\not{1}\,{}^{1}001 \Rightarrow {}^{0}\!\!\not{1}\,{}^{9}\!\!\not{0}\,{}^{1}01 \Rightarrow {}^{0}\!\!\not{1}\,{}^{9}\!\!\not{0}\,{}^{9}\!\!\not{0}\,{}^{1}1$$

$$- \ 107 \qquad - \ 1 \ 07 \qquad - \ 1 \ \ 0 \ 7$$

$$8 \quad 9 \ 4$$

6. 14

   $39 - 25 = 14$

7. 11

   $23 - 12 = 11$

8. 93

   $132 - 93$. This may have been tough, because you were trying to find out the difference and you may not have known it was subtraction. But whenever you are looking for the difference between 2 numbers, subtraction is the way to find it. In fact, the answer to a subtraction problem is called a difference.

9. 78

   $117 - 39 = 78$. Here you had to borrow, and it might have gotten complicated. But to check your work, just add back. Does the answer plus 39 equal 117? If not, you need to change it.

10. 872

   You can add the detective novels and science fiction together first: $40 + 100 = 140$ detective novels and science fiction. Then subtract: $1,012 - 140 = 872$. Or you could subtract twice: $1,012 - 40 = 972$ and then $972 - 100 = 872$.

MULTIPLICATION REVIEW

1. 40

2. 42

3. 238

   Did you remember that to multiply by 10, you can just add a 0 to the end of the number?

4. 322

   Did you approximate first? Try 23 times 10 is 230, and 23 times 20 is 460, so 23 times 14 is somewhere in between those two.

5. 12,408

6. 10 books

   $2 \times 5 = 10$

7. 70 jellybeans

   $10 \times 7 = 70$

8. 100 spiders

   $10 \times 10 = 100$. Remember: just add a 0 when you multiply by 10.

9. 726 racecars

   $22 \times 33 = 726$. How close was your approximation?

10. 4,429 buttons total

    $103 \times 43 = 4,429$. To approximate, try 40 times 100. Since you multiply by 100, add two zeros. A 40 with two zeros is 4,000, which is way more than 1,000.

DIVISION REVIEW

1. 2

2. 8

3. 9 r1

    $3 \times 9 = 27$, and then the extra 1 of 28 is the remainder.

4. 22

5. 11

6. 2 pictures on each wall

    You could even draw a picture of the room and the walls if that makes it easier for you. Eight pictures divided among 4 walls is $8 \div 4$, which equals 2.

7. 4 bugs per board

    Whenever you have trouble deciding which number is being divided into, ask yourself which amount is being separated into groups. The

32 bugs are being divided among 8 boards, so the equation should be $32 \div 8$, which is equal to 4.

8. 8 sandwiches each, with 3 left over

There are 35 sandwiches and 4 people eating (Sondra *and* her 3 friends). The sandwiches are being divided up among the friends, so $35 \div 4$, which equals 8 r3.

9. 25 shirts per drawer

The 225 shirts are being separated into groups to be put into drawers, so $225 \div 9 = 25$.

10. Each child will get 22 teeth.

How can you approximate here? Well, there are about 350 teeth, and about 15 kids. If each kid got 10 teeth, that's 150, so twice that, or 20 teeth each, is about 300. There are more teeth than 300, right? So each kid will get more than 20. $352 \div 16 = 22$.

ABOUT THE AUTHORS

Marcia Lerner graduated from Brown University in 1986. She is the author of *Writing Smart* and *Math Smart,* and has been teaching and writing for The Princeton Review since 1988. She lives in Brooklyn, New York.

Doug McMullen Jr. is a writer who has, among other things, worked for the circus and harvested wildflowers. He has been teaching for The Princeton Review since 1988.

Carolyn Wheater teaches middle school and upper school mathematics at the Nightingale-Bamford School in New York City. Educated at Marymount Manhattan College and the University of Massachusetts—Amherst, she has taught math and computer technology for 30 years to students from preschool through college.